texture

.......a closer look

Lois Ericson

Photos: Laura Gregersen
                    (unless noted)
Illustrations: Linda Taynahza
Calligraphy: Mary Street
Editor: Lennart Ericson

dedication

To Jane Chapman, who opened my eyes to the wonderful world of art . . .

To Patty Bogstie White who encouraged me to keep sewing, and guided me through my first successful sewing projects . . .

Special thanks to Mary Street, typist, and Susan Genevich, model.

Cover fabric: Author

Printed in Hong Kong for Eric's Press

ISBN 0-911985-04-2

Ideas are everywhere.
Everything exists in
the universe.
Come... Take it...
If you can.

Plato

foreword

Everyone reading this book shares a common bond..
. the love of fibers and threads. We are all involved
in the world of texture--nubby, rough, bumpy,
smooth, shaggy, slick, organic, grainy, lumpy.

Textile artists are especially fortunate because they
can translate this wonderful world of texture to
threads and fabrics, making them exciting to see and
exciting to feel. They take the ordinary and make it
extraordinary. They take the mundane and make it
stimulating. They take the monotonous and make it
exhilarating. Best of all, they have fun!

Lois Ericson has gathered together a sampling of
work from a variety of textile artists across the
country.   She shares with us their work, their
inspirations, and their ideas, as well as her own.
Now it is YOUR turn to adapt techniques from this
book to YOUR threads and YOUR fabrics. Create for
yourself a more interesting world in which to live.
 Most important, enjoy!

Jerry Zarbaugh, Editor
Aardvark Territorial Enterprize

content

Introduction.............................6
Process..................................7
Chapter Preview...................... 8
Inspiration
      Radiators............................ 9
      Church............................. 19
      Statue.............................. 29
      Building............................ 37
      Wire................................ 43
      Leaves............................. 49
      Cornice............................57
      Pod.................................63
      Rock wall.........................71
      Cars................................ 79
Color.................................... 87
Work....................................103
      Chapter Preview.................. 104
Chapter Preview, techniques........... 178
Techniques............................. 179
      Wrinkled/stitched 180
      Piecing 182
      Stitching........................ 184
      Tucks............................ 186
      Cording.......................... 188
      Piping........................... 189
      Faced Shapes..................... 190
      Shaped Insets.................... 194
      Shirring......................... 195
      Smocking 196
      Tubes............................ 198
      Stabilizer....................... 201
      Marbeling........................ 202
      Papermaking 203
      Felting 204
Just a word 205
Artists................................ 206
      Chapter Preview.................. 207
Suppliers.............................. 220
Bibliography........................... 221
Index.................................. 222
Quote.................................. 224

introduction

This is a collection of work from many friends, some of whom I've yet to meet in person. For the most part, cloth is the medium used to express their art. In some cases, fiber is used, as in felting or papermaking.

The visual and tactile quality of a surface results from the way in which the materials are used. So, in this book, it is with pleasure that I share the ideas and techniques that comprise the dimensional surface.

I hope that the ideas presented will be thought provoking, a starting point for imagined possibilities.

. . . A place to begin.

process

We can be inspired by and create the textures that we see in our everyday world. Minute details can be more important than the whole. . . sometimes exquisite and complete . . . so consider isolating one section of a photo or drawing. Awareness and an inherent curiosity may help us to connect with the textured surface to be investigated and interpreted.

To create exciting work, it cannot be borrowed intact from nature. The artist must use imagination to solve a problem, to express an idea....at the same time considering the materials to be used. The restriction or freedom of the medium and/or materials chosen contributes to the variety of pieces with the same initial inspiration.

The same familiar shapes can stimulate many people to express different ideas. The participants, in this section of the book have all been challenged by the same photos, i.e. to translate the realistic objects to texture using their particular medium.

The photographer had a great eye when she took this photo of the stack of old radiators at the junk-yard. It certainly evoked a lot responses by the fiber enthusiasts.

Material: Corduroy, linen/cotton, moire taffeta
Technique: The exercise in these two examples was to investigate and experiment with a variety of tucks and pleats. Soft pleats--stitched in place, pintucks, tucks shown on the wrong side. When combining an assortment of fabrics with one technique, the possibilities multiply.
Work: Karen Perrine

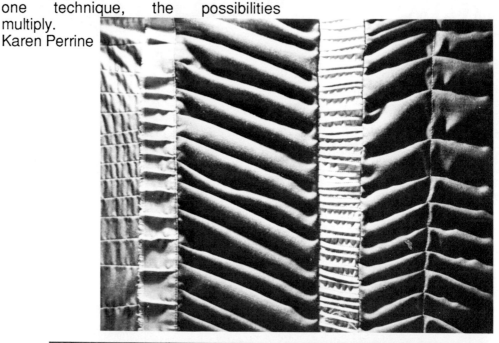

This interpretation combines tucks and pleats with several interesting materials. The tucks were stitched on the moire then turned to the other side, so it looks like darts. These tucked pieces were then cut up and sewn back together at various angles.

Material: Paper, silk, glue
Technique: 2" strips of various papers including foil
                and some silk fabric . . . were dyed,
                others were purchased for the texture
                and color.   These strips were then
                wrapped around a knitting needle and
                glued.
Work: Anne Syer

Materials: Cotton muslin, India ink

Technique: The fabric has been painted with an
                ink wash, when dry it was run
                through a pleater.

Work: Caty Carlin   13

Material: Fiberglass screening, staples, silver thread
Technique: The forms represented folded paper accordians that were made by children. This construction idea was the starting point and the screening was the medium. The screening was cut in large pieces or in strips . . . some were painted. The accordian folded strips were held together visually and constructively with staples and silver thread.
Work: Ardi Davis

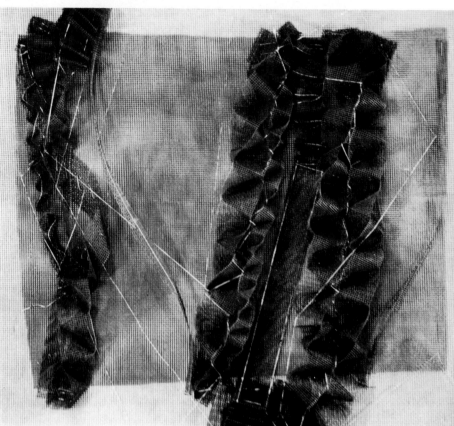

How to fold strips into accordians.

Fold long strips in half at right angles.

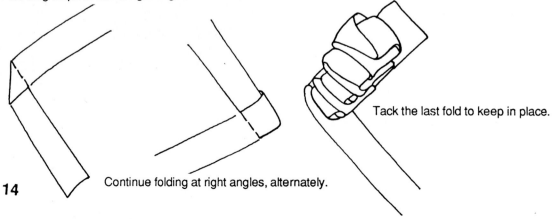

Tack the last fold to keep in place.

Continue folding at right angles, alternately.

14

Material: Gold metallic knit
Technique: The fabric is wrinkled/stitched and quilted. Many, many small squares, like little pillows, are stuffed and stacked next to each other. The nature of the metallic material is such that it disperses and reflects the light . . . good choice of fabric. Notice below the isolated section that was chosen to interpret.
Work: Emelyn Garafolo

Material: Cotton, plain and striped
Technique: There were 10 different striped cottons
              from pin stripes to 1 1/2" wide ones,
              used in this effective interpretation.
              Some of the smocking sections were
              pleated on the smocking/pleater and
              some were pleated by hand, when the
              size of the pleats were varied.   The
              pleated pieces were stitched to a
              background material and then machine
              satin stitched in black.
Work: B.J. Adams

Materials:	Cotton, batting
Technique:	Piecing and quilting techniques combine in this all cotton example stitched in shades of mauve, lavender with cream. The linear quality of strip piecing emphasizes the shapes of the inspirational photograph.
Work:	Laura Reinstatler

Material: Cotton, linen, batting
Technique: The various fabrics were tucked and pleated. These were then cut up and sewn back together with covered piping inserted in the seams. Some of the sections were stuffed and some were quilted.
Work: Lorraine Torrence

The church steeple was the more popular image, interpretations ranged from realistic to very abstract.

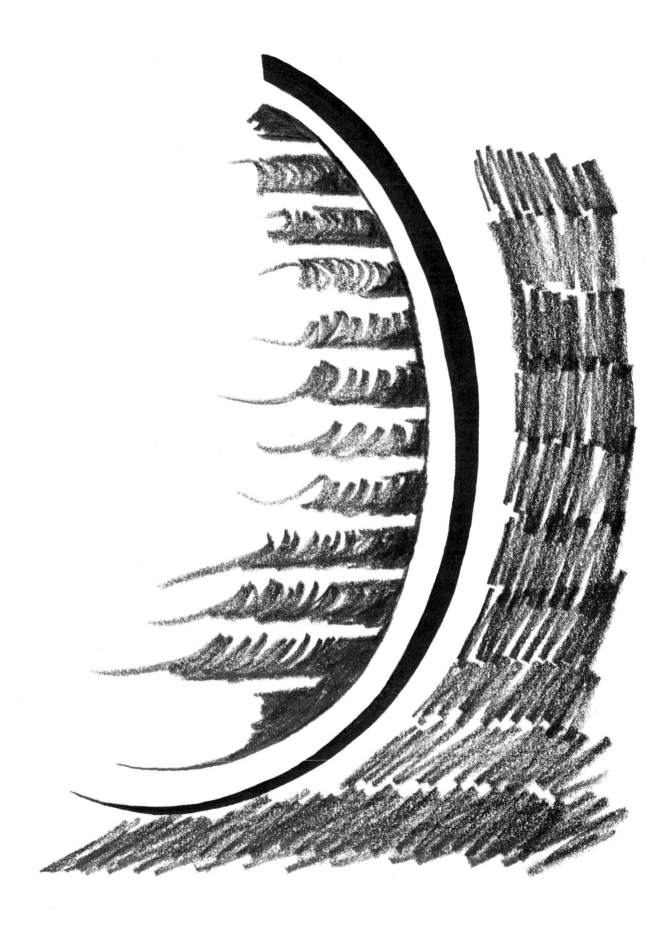

Material: Cotton, striped and plain, plus black
             organza
Technique: Cut pieces were covered with organza
             and stitched through all layers . .
             outlining all the shapes. Think about it .
             .. great idea! Any cut shapes can just
             be placed next to each other, no
             finishing! After the organza is placed
             on top, the stitching holds everything
             together . . . Looking like very intricate
             applique.

             The photo was enlarged, the copies cut
             up and rearranged . . . fine abstract
             design.   The isolated square, see
             below, is the portion that was
             interpreted.
Work: Lynne Sward

Material: Cotton fabric
Technique: Flat turned tubes are stitched to a
              backing. Some are folded, these could
              also be corded for a more rounded
              effect.
Work: Caty Carlin

Material: Striped cotton
Technique: The tucks have been stitched to show
              the various colors of the stripes. These
              tucks have then been manipulated and
              fastened with machine satin stitching.
              Notice that the direction of the tucks in
              some of the circles changes.   The
              circles have been cut out and those
              edges have been covered with the
              wider rows of machine satin stitching.
Work: B.J. Adams

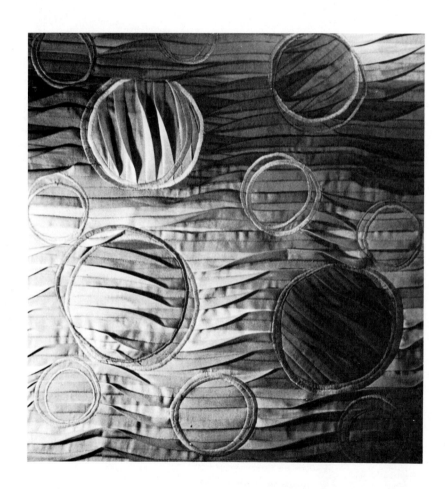

The circular shape on the church
became the starting point for several
pieces.

Material: Cotton, prints and plain also 'slick pen' fabric paint for diagonal stripes.

Technique: The tucks on the background have been done with a double needle over cording. The center circle has pin tucks combined with a print fastened with satin stitching. The 'slick pen' makes very puffy lines and comes in pastel colors.

Work: Linda Kimura Rees

These two interpretations are by the
same person. After doing the realistic
piece, the artist decided to try a more
abstract one.

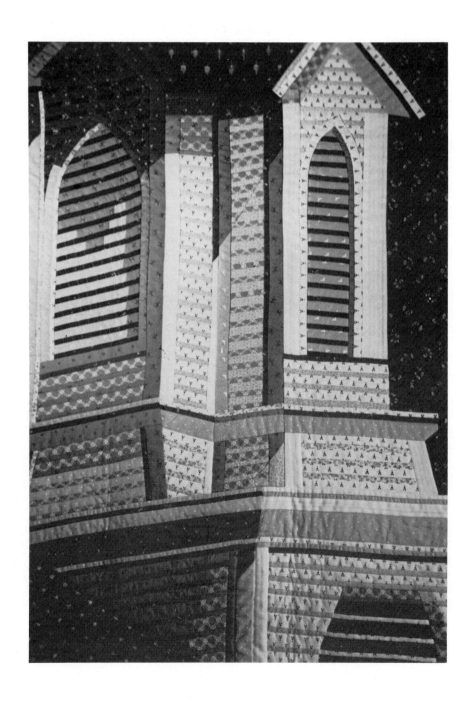

Material: Cotton, prints and plain, also cording and batting
Technique: Piecing and quilting are the main methods used on these two pieces. The sections that appear to be striped are <u>very</u> narrow strips of two different fabrics . . . pieced. Some corded piping is inserted in the more abstract sample.
Work: Laura Reinstatler

Material: Printed and plain cottons and batting
Technique: This example was pieced using a
variety of cottons.   Tucking, quilting
and a lot of stitching . . . some with a
double needle . . . were used in
combination.
Work: Lois Smith

Statue made of stone, yet it seems to be soft....it would be interesting to think about working on a series with that kind of feeling.

29

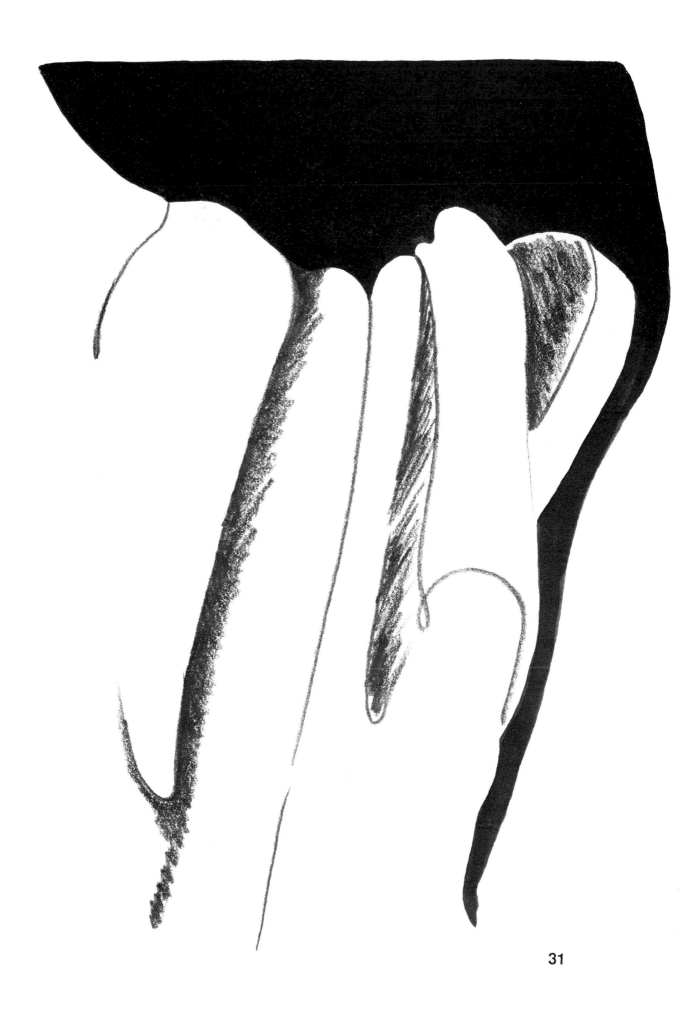

Materials: Cotton muslin

Technique: Stitching lines to make a grid pattern using thinner material, gives a different effect, especially when stitched on the diagonal.

Work: Karen Perrine

Material: Cotton velveteen
Technique: Two layers of fabric were pinned
together on one edge, then parallel
lines were sewn on the fabric, with the
top layer moved to make a 'tunnel'.
After all the 'tunnels' were sewn, cross
lines were sewn so that a little pleat
formed every time a stitched line was
crossed.
Work: Karen Perrine

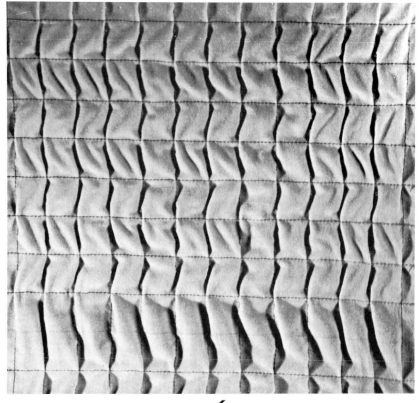

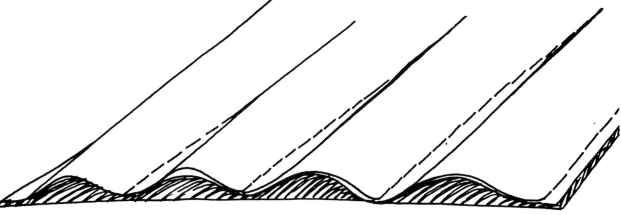

'tunnels' as described

A wide range of fabrics available has a great effect on the results of our work. The satin on the sample below has so much life to it, in contrast to the knit fabric, opposite, which seems to recede.

Material: Satin
Technique: An iron-on interfacing was used giving extra body to this heavy slipper satin. A two inch grid was drawn on the back. The smocking pattern was stitched on the back of the fabric by machine, see Techniques.
Work: B.J. Adams

Material: Cotton knit
Technique: The knit fabric has been stitched, then
             draped and pulled until the soft pleats
             occurred.   The row was stitched in
             place.   The cloth is then moved in the
             opposite direction and stitched again.
Work: Author

Materials: Cotton voile and broadcloth plus batting

Technique: Voile, gauze, organza are fabrics to consider for this technique. Layer the material as follows: backing, batting, black broadcloth, topped by three layers of voile. A pattern is stitched through all layers, then some of these sheer layers are cut away.

Work: Pat Rodgers

The windows and the angles of the buildings, combined with the texture of the bricks, make this a good design challenge.

Material: Cotton muslin
Technique: The major masses were traced from the photo and enlarged. The forms were built up with folded and painted muslin strips. These pieces were then layered, rolled, and folded into points. The work was painted with a black wash.
Work: Ardi Davis

Material: Cotton, linen, silk organza, canvas
Technique: The section at the top has been pleated, and stitched in place. The facing of organza casts a shadow around the windows. All the stitching threads are left on top as part of the design.
Work: Author

Material: Cotton
Technique: Various sized tucks are stitched on this
             cotton fabric. The pieces are then cut
             and pieced together with plain cloth.
Work: Lorraine Torrence

Wide blades of grass are juxtaposed with barbed wire in this interesting photograph. Good combination of background shadows, directional lines with the metal of the fence.

Material: Cotton, batting, paint
Technique: One small section of the barbed wire was enlarged for this painted design. The cotton fabric was then quilted to emphasize the motif. This is a great example of simplifying an idea. . . a good exercise that most of us could explore.
Work: Mary Street

Material: Netting, mesh, printed cotton, ribbon
Technique: Machine stitching both straight and satin . . . in various widths . . . accentuates the pieces that are applied to a cotton background.
Work: Nancy Smeltzer

Material: Canvas background, with linen and cotton

Technique: First of all, the photo was turned sideways . . calligraphic images seemed to appear. The wide blades were painted with a spongy brush and very little paint. The 'letters' were cut out and facings applied, then turned.

Work: Author

The overlapping leaves in this photograph appear to be made of organza or some other sheer fabric.

50

Material: Cotton linter, plant pulp, paint
Technique: The paper pulp was combined with the hardening agent and spooned onto wrinkled aluminum foil. When dried, the leaves were painted with Luma watercolors. For basic handmade paper method see Techniques.
Work: Barbi Racich

Material: Cotton Batiste, 'solvy'
Technique: Machine cutwork and needlelace are the methods used in this free stitchery sample. Sheer fabric is fastened to 'solvy'* ...by pinning, basting or by using a glue stick or spray adhesive. When the embroidery is finished . . wet the backing and it does indeed dissolve, see Techniques.
Work: Pat Rodgers

Material: Paper, glue, dye
Technique: This bowl was made of dyed paper. The paper was layered including some silk threads, over a ceramic bowl to shape. It was then coated with diluted white glue. This technique would also lend itself to sheer fabrics. The effect of the light shining through the layers of these bowls is similar to the veins of the leaves.
Work: Anne Syer

Material: Cotton print
Technique: A muted printed cotton is the
             background fabric. The stitching, over
             cotton crochet ·thread, was done with a
             double needle.
Work: Linda Kimura Rees

Materials: Unspun wool fleece, silk jacquard, cotton bias tape and cord

Technique: The fleece has been couched by machine stitching, to keep it in place . . other patterns, i.e. a grid, could also be used. I like the look of the fleece, but other materials could be considered, some that could be hand washed or dry cleaned, if this were to be used on a garment.

Work: Lois Ericson

The paint has started to peel off the cornice and the wood joints are separating....the nails and nail holes are very visible. The deterioration of the building enhances the angles.

59

Material: Cotton broadcloth, pillow ticking
Technique: Torn strips of pillow ticking are
              combined with a small print. All the
              pieces are zigzagged in place.
Work: Mary Preston

Material: Canvas background, polyester crepe
Technique: The crepe fabric was cut in long strips
              and stitched to form tubes. These were
              turned, pressed and stitched onto the
              background.
Work: Author

Material: Cotton broadcloth, metallic thread
Technique: Tucks were stitched in the cotton fabric and combined with strip patchwork. Turned tubes were applied and the metallic thread was couched in place.
Work: Author

A common milkweed pod
has many textures -- from
soft, fluffly to prickly, hard.

Material: Cotton fabric and batting
Technique: This sample was quilted and pieced. . .
             the strips are about 1/4" finished
             pieces.   This approach to interpreting
             the photo is very abstract. Piecing has
             a way of reducing curved shapes to
             straight lines and angles.
Work: Laura Reinstatler

Material: Cotton chintz, batting, threads
Technique: French knots and the couching are all
              accomplished on the sewing machine.
              The batting emphasizes the rounded
              pattern of the stitching lines.
Work: Pat Rodgers

MACHINE KNOT

Stitch width 2 1/2 to 3 1/2, length 0
1. Bar tack to build up thread -
2. Bar tack over center, across first tack +
3. Now starting at center, bar tack to ends
   on top of #1

Material: Silk
Technique: Dyed strips of silk are fringed and
             layered.   The various weaves of silk
             take the dyes and fringe . . . differently.
             The fringe is just the 'feeling' of the soft
             'umbrellas' of the pod.
Work: Anne Syer

Material: Open mesh, thread, cotton background
Technique: The mesh, lower right of photo below, was placed in a hoop. Elastic thread was wound on the bobbin and the pattern stitched. When the hoop was removed, the cloth contracts. The result was a 'bumpy' texture.
Work: Lois Smith

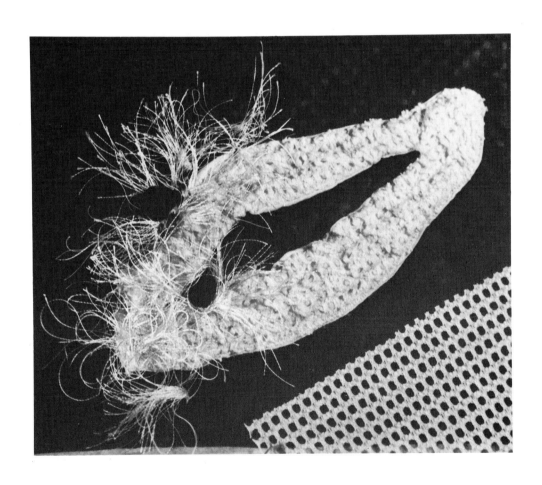

Material: Paper pulp, pine cone, unspun fleece
Technique: Handmade paper is molded by layering
              the pulp on a framework, in this case,
              the pine cone.
Work: Barbi Racich

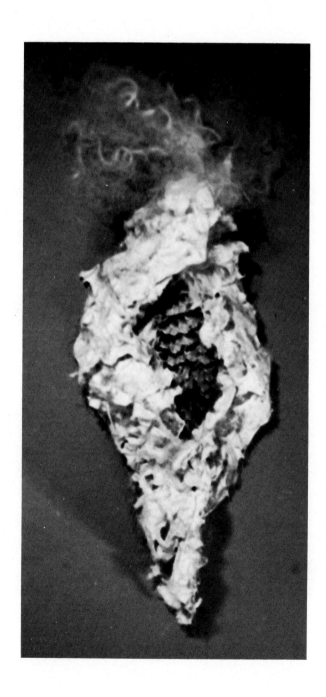

This rock surface has a lot of action going on even though it is a relatively flat plane. Notice the shadows cast by the extended shapes.

73

Material: Cotton, black paint
Technique: The sharp edges of the shadows cast
              by the rocks were interpreted by cutting
              the painted cloth and mounting it on a
              black background. Small strips of white
              fabric were crimped and woven
              through the slit areas.
Work: Mary Ann Caplinger

Material: Cotton linters, paint
Technique: Paper pulp has been molded and shaped, then painted in this interpretation of the rock wall. If you haven't tried making paper, it certainly is a technique to consider.
Work: Ingrid Evans

Material: Cotton, batting
Technique: The vertical lines and shadows are
             interpreted in a combination of
             Seminole patchwork, strip piecing,
             quilting and soft pleats.
Work: Laura Reinstatler

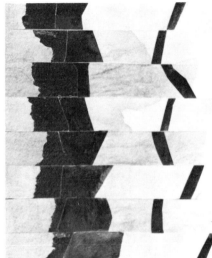

Material: Paper, silk and foil
Technique: To achieve a shadow effect was the purpose of these samples. To get this effect dyed paper, silk and foil were torn and overlapped. These large constructed pieces were then cut into strips. The movement of the strips is the same as Seminole patchwork. The artist used these maquettes as 'sketches' for larger pieces .
Work: Anne Syer

Material: Cotton, plain and prints
Technique: Torn and cut strips of fabric are layered
             and stitched in place. . . some sheer
             pieces of cloth are adding a little
             dimension and shadow . . . bits of
             threads and yarns also add interest.
Work: Mary Preston

The horizontal lines of the crushed, stacked cars were apparent in all of the interpretations.

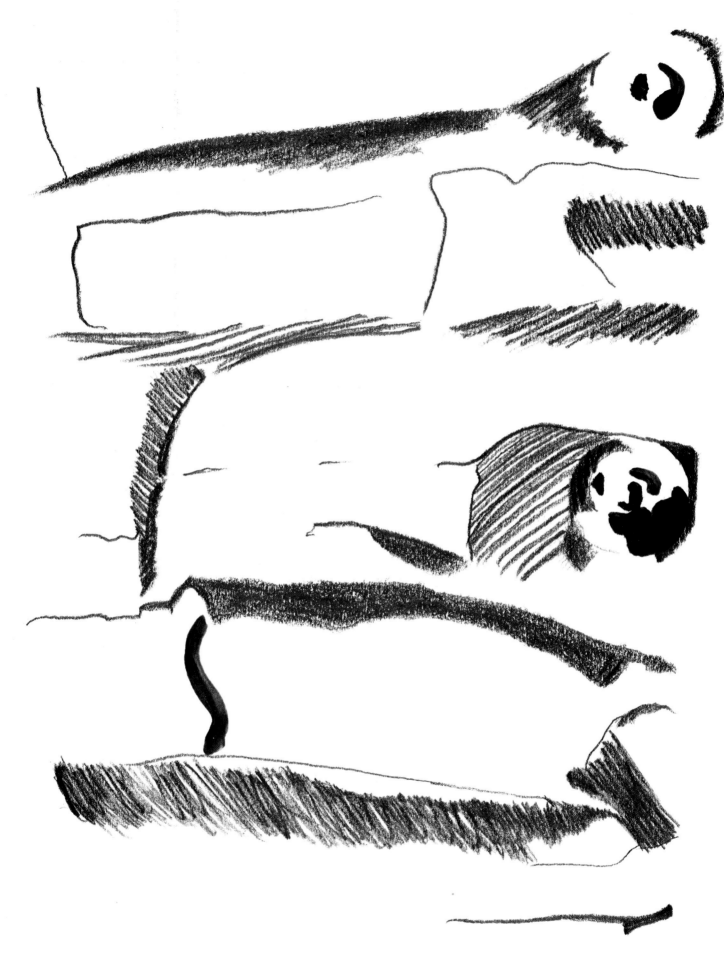

Material: Cottons, plain and striped
Technique: Tucks were sewn, then pressed and stitched. Turned tubes of fabric were twisted together. Piping and shirring were used to complete this sample.
Work: Liz Thoman

Materials: White cotton muslin, India ink, cording
Technique: An abstract design was painted on the muslin. The manipulated cloth looks like many rows of piping -- possible but tedious. The cording was placed between two layers of fabric, the one underneath stays flat, the painted piece on top is undulating to accommodate the cording. Use a zipper foot to make the rows of stitching tight.

Work: Caty Carlin

Material: Satin, taffeta, cotton, buttons, cording
Technique: Soft pleating and piping are combined with quilted tubes of various fabrics in this solution.
Work: Lois Smith

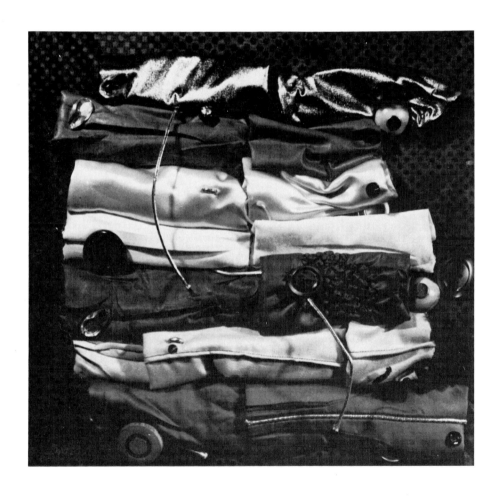

Material: Cottons, plain and printed
Technique: Machine stitching, make a pattern and keep the wrinkled fabric in place. Facings on some of the shapes create interest and movement.
Work: Mary Preston

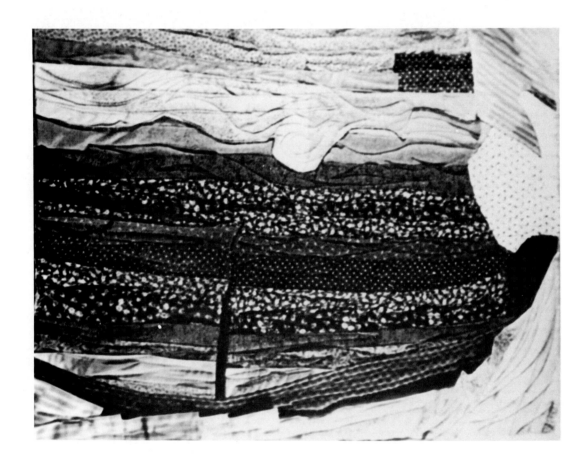

Material: Cotton. . . black and grey stripes (1 1/2"
            wide)
Technique: The wide stripes were ironed into box
            pleats, then satin stitched in three
            shades of grey thread, also black. This
            would work well for a garment perhaps
            with the pleats left open in appropriate
            places.
Work: B.J. Adams

Material: Plain and ribbed knits
Technique: Tubes and flat strips are machine
             zigzagged, a serger could also be
             used. The rippled edges are made by
             stretching the knit as it is sewn. After
             copying and enlarging the photo, the
             artist connected the images with
             bamboo.
Work: Emelyn Garafolo

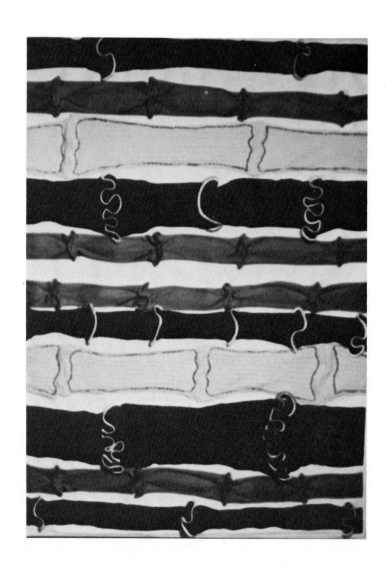

Anne Syer

87

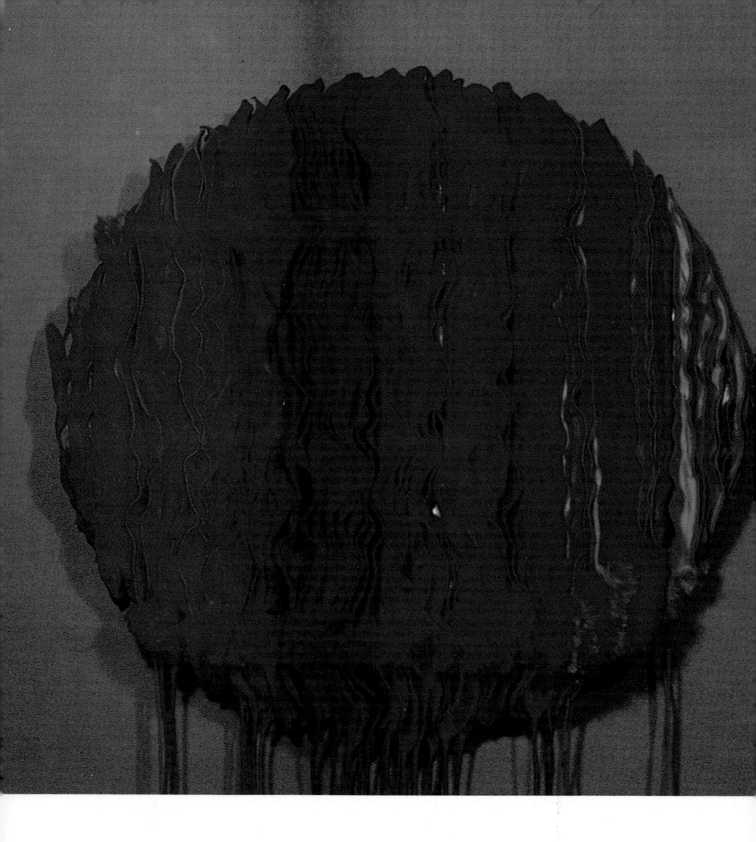

Emelyn Garafolo

Lynne Sward

89

Lois Ericson
90

Caty Carlin
91

Gayle Luchessa

92

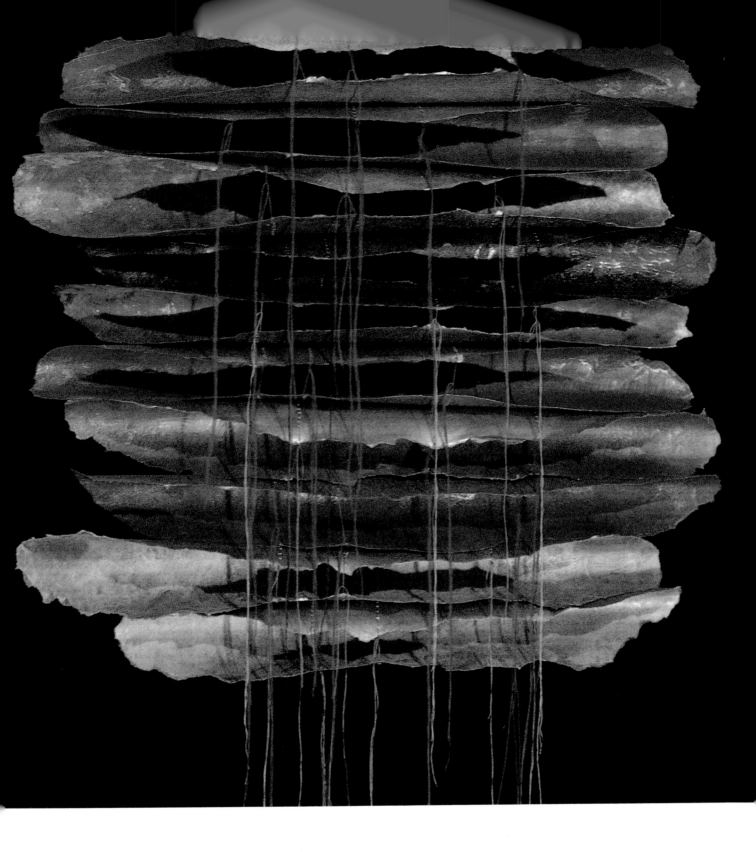

Barbi Racich

93

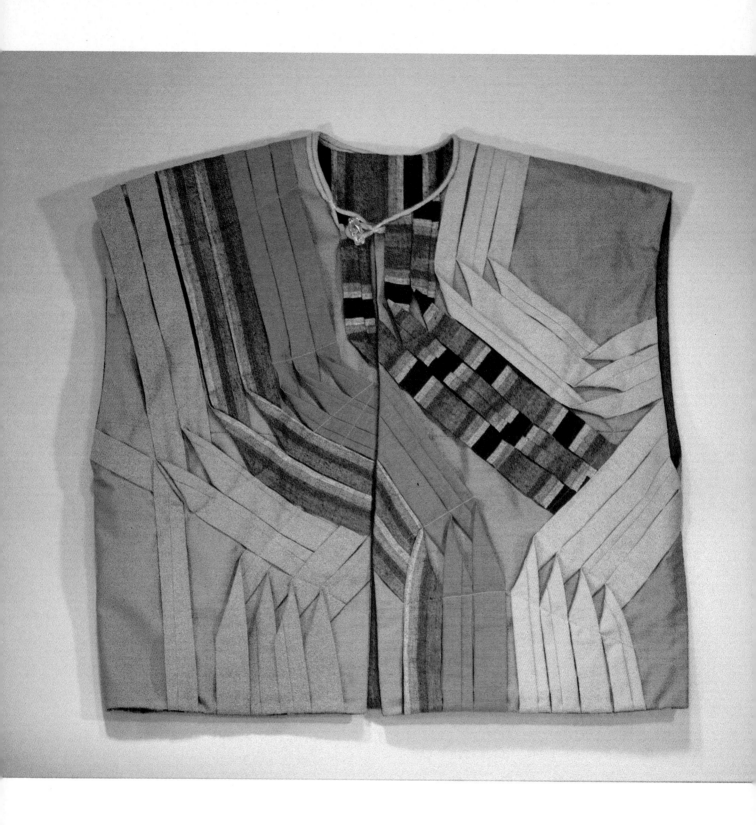

Lois Ericson

94

Mary Preston

95

Laura Reinstatler

96

Ardi Davis

97

B.J. Adams

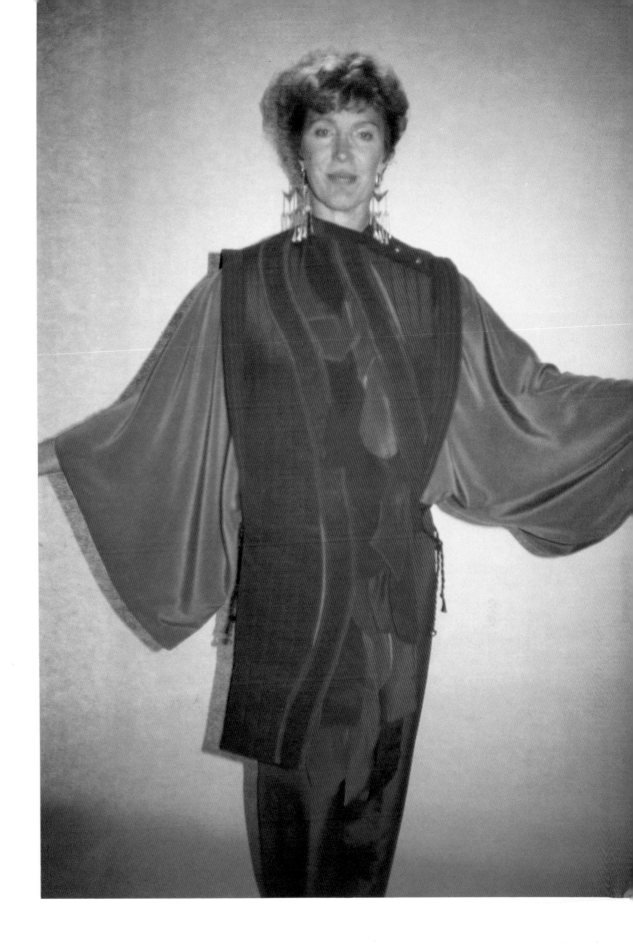

Lois Ericson

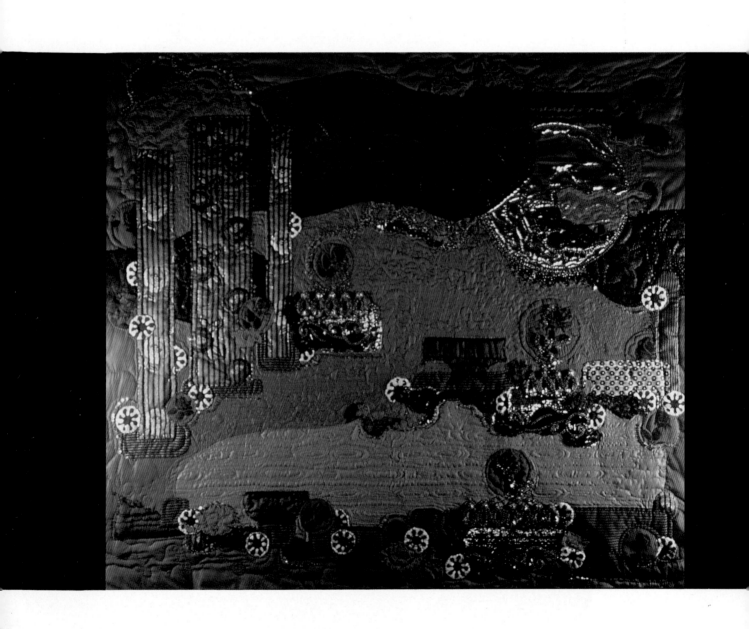

Nancy Smeltzer

100

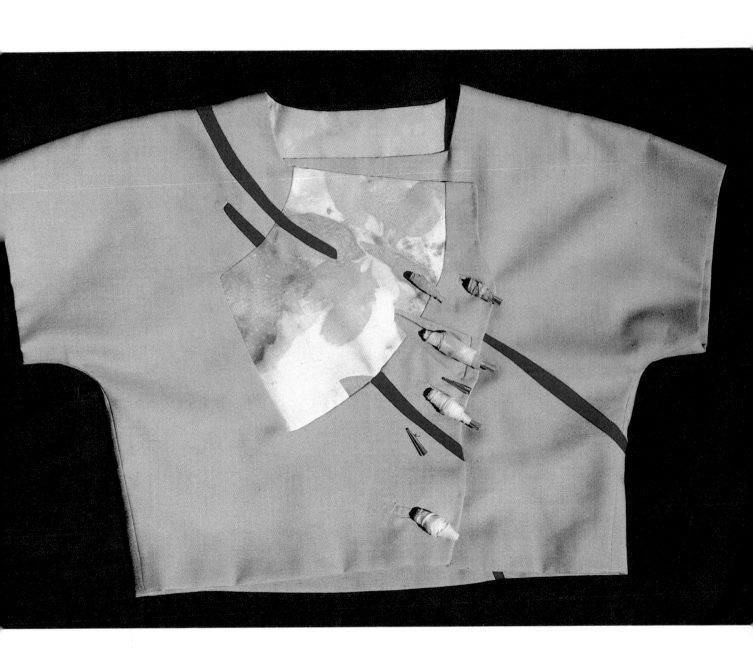

Ingrid Evans
102

work

_____ from texture
. . . . to finished pieces

I'd like to share part of a letter from Emelyn, one of the participants in the book. As I read the comments, I connected immediately with the attitudes expressed. . . . maybe you will, too .

"My background was surface design, but there was an unrest there with the limitations of 'flat pattern'. I had long been excited by bas reliefs; so I began padding and quilting--a move in that direction. I became intrigued with the possibility of pushing the inherent qualities of cloth beyond these limitations. . . My interest in 'fabric manipulation' (I now had a name for it) developed into a full blown addiction, and is now beginning to move toward sculpture."

I especially liked the use of the term . . . unrest. That was well put. In my case, understated!

In seminars, I'm frequently asked . . . "How can I create my own individual style?" To find our 'style' is not a conscious effort or the purpose of working. I have found that when one produces a great amount of work. . . a particular style has just evolved. The artists represented in this section each have their own recognizable style.

These are pieces from the artists' collections (or in the collections of others, as indicated) in which texture is the common element.

The title of this piece is 'Panache'. . . the units consist of two layers of bias strips of varying lengths. The rippled effect comes from the bias cut, combined with the close zigzagging stitch that holds the two layers together. The areas of 'cloud shadows' were ravelled instead of zigzagged. These strips were stitched down the center onto a backing grid. The feathers and the feather-shaped strips are connected to the sun with wrapped parallel cords that are tacked together at various points.

Photo & Work: Emelyn Garafolo

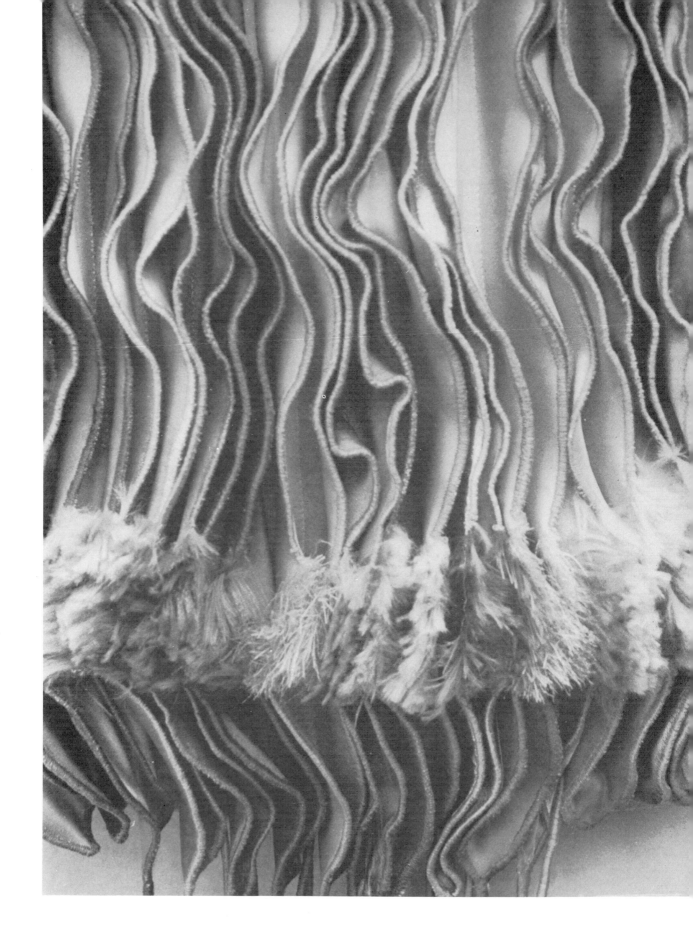

Many strips were torn and/or folded lengthwise, off center to allow one edge to show below the other, on this piece called "Image".

A nice shadow effect can be made by using this method using a variety of fabrics, i.e., sheers combined with other cloth textures.

These torn strips are stitched on the fold to a background grid in overlapping rows. Some of the strips are bias cut and zigzagged at the edges.

Photo & Work ： Emelyn Garafolo

On this piece called 'Daystar' the strips were cut on the bias of satin and taffeta. Each strip is comprised of two colors--yellow and white--that are sewn together at the edge with two rows of very tight zigzagging. The colors of the threads used are varied on some of the strips.

The strips are sewn down the center onto the background grid. The 'Sun' area was created by pulling two edges of the same strip together for a limited distance and zigzagging over both edges. This created a 'pocket' which hides the inside (yellow) up to the area where it opens to reveal the top surface. The 'shadow' of the sun is a change of color of thread used on the taffeta, plus ironing it in the proper direction.

Photo & Work : Emelyn Garafolo

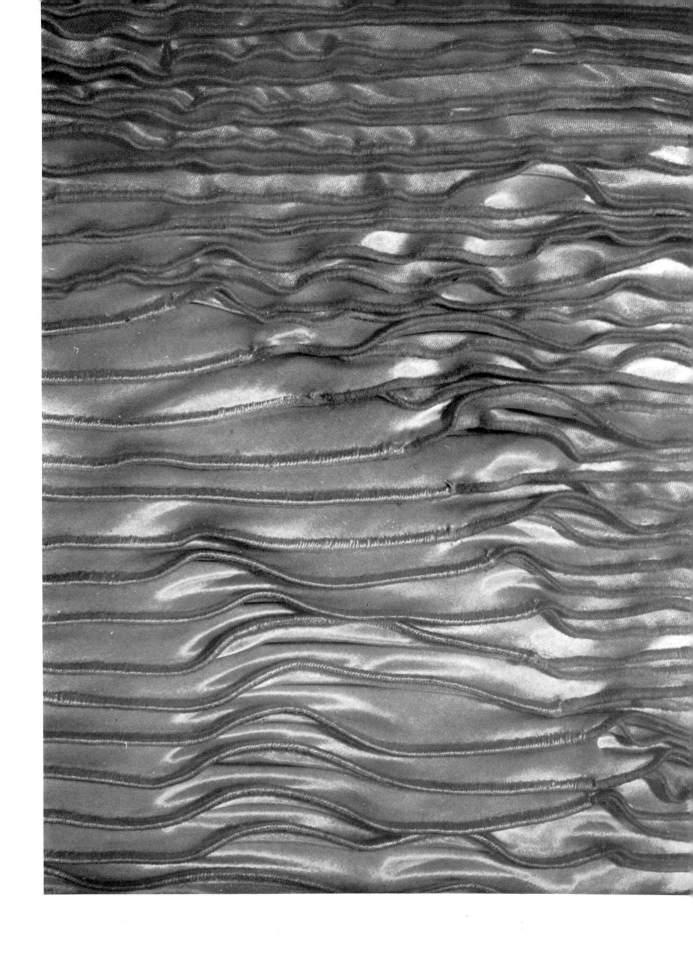

The textures on this close-up were made by using various sizes of covered cording. The corded pieces were done by sewing successive pieces of piping next to the preceeding piece. Each piece was sewn onto the seam allowance of the last piece. In some places a plain piece of fabric was sewn next to a cord, then stuffed to make a big shape, then 'sealed' with the next piece of piping. Some small inserted shapes were first sewn and stuffed, then stitched down with the next piece of piping.

Many of the textured fabrics were dyed to produce subtle differences in the shading. The whole piece was attached to a thin piece of wood for easy hanging.

Photo & Work : Lorraine Torrance

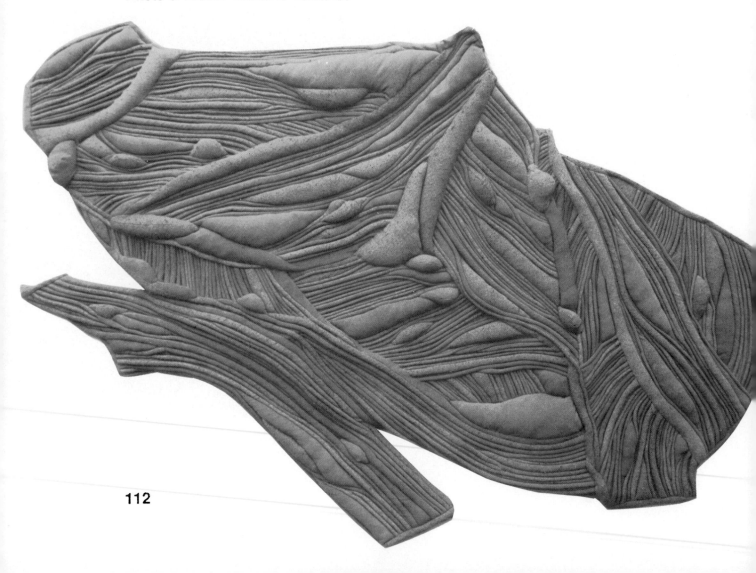

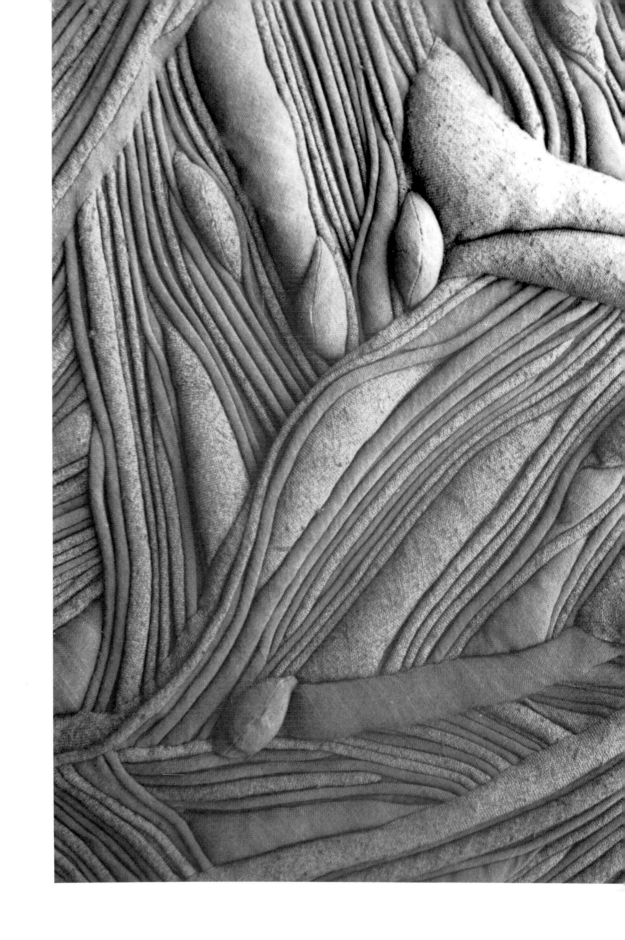

Lynne Sward calls this technique 'scatter and sew' and she says she is very excited about it. . . . I would be too! I have used scraps in a variety of ways, but this one is just terrific! She sorts her scraps into general color groups, cutting pieces smaller if necessary. She places the scraps onto the background fabric and stitches them in place, criss-crossing the rows of stitches to keep all in place.

These works are mounted on padded boards. The fibers are a mixture of cottons, blends, silks and sometimes paper.

She says she feels that her work has taken on a painterly effect and by using the letter combinations it encourages the viewer to come to their own conclusions about what she is trying to say.

Work & Photo : Lynne Sward

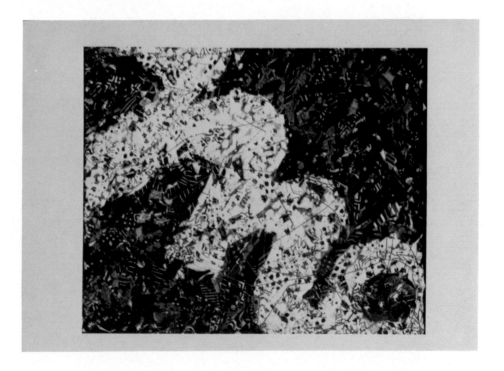

When I first saw Laura Reinstatler's work , I was very impressed, from a distance, the quilt seemed to be made of small ribbons. As I walked closer I discovered that indeed it was really made of very narrow strips pieced together. The finished width of the strips appears to be about 1/4". Incredible! Also her color sense is so delicate and sensitive, great addition to all the other pieces represented here.

The minute piecing is clearly seen on the right. After sewing the strips together, they are then re-cut in some instances and resewn. Long strips are divided with plain strips of cloth, or made into what appears to be a checkerboard. The quilts either for the wall, the bed, or the body are usually made of cotton. (In the collection of Dr. Phillip Frank.)

Work: Laura Reinstatler
Photo: Ken Wagner

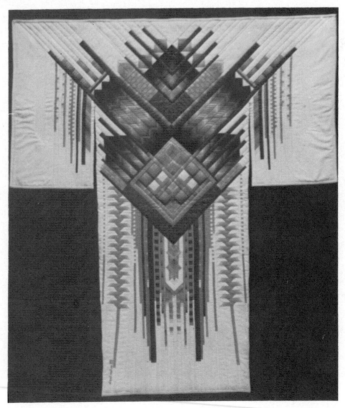

When I first saw the picture of this vest . . . it reminded me of the clothes, from centuries past, that were slashed to show other fabrics underneath (that originated from seeing the uniforms after battle that were cut and torn).

This vest was cut out and then painted in free form design. The vest was quilted . . . the outside and the lining sewn together. The threads from the quilting were pulled to the outside, tied and left uncut for added texture. Narrow bias strips that were attached with beads add dimension and further embellish this cotton vest. This piece is called "Out on a Limb".

Work: Mary Preston
Photo: Monika Young

This coat was cut from a plain piece of medium weight white canvas material. It was painted with wide brushes. . . house painting brushes were excellent for this purpose. Mary wanted to express the movement of light breaking through the darkness, she said. The light streak was drizzled on with a squeeze bottle. She also painted the cotton/acryllic string with the same color as the light streak and applied it to the coat with transparent thread and a zigzag stitch. This string was also applied in the same way to parts of the lining and the inside banding. The main colors are purple and yellow. The piece is called 'Winter Survival/Affirmations'.

Work: Mary Preston
Photo: Monika Young

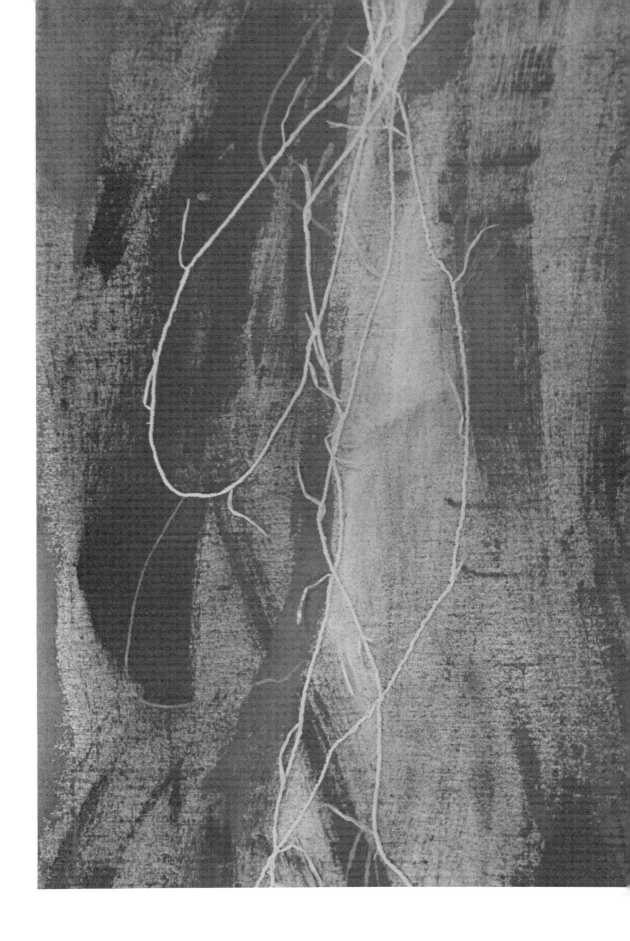

One large piece of fabric is folded and tacked to a backing material in a pattern that seems to have a lot of movement. Each row seemingly enveloping the next. There is an inquisitive interest in the technique of how the connecting and folding occurs. This is the kind of curiosity that points towards experminenting and usually leads to a whole new series of work. Also notice the loose threads that add a subtle dimension.

Work: Ardi Davis
Photo: F2 Photography

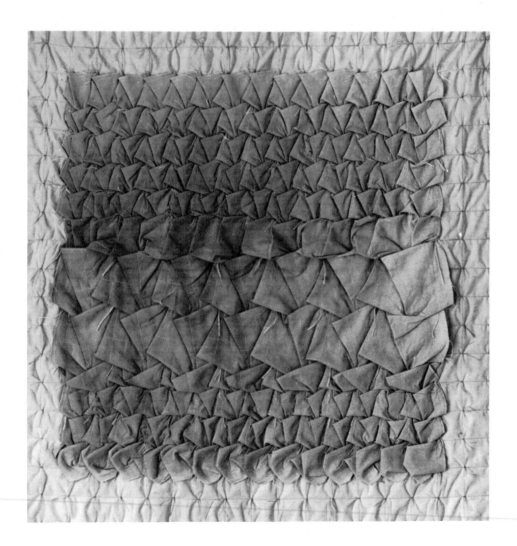

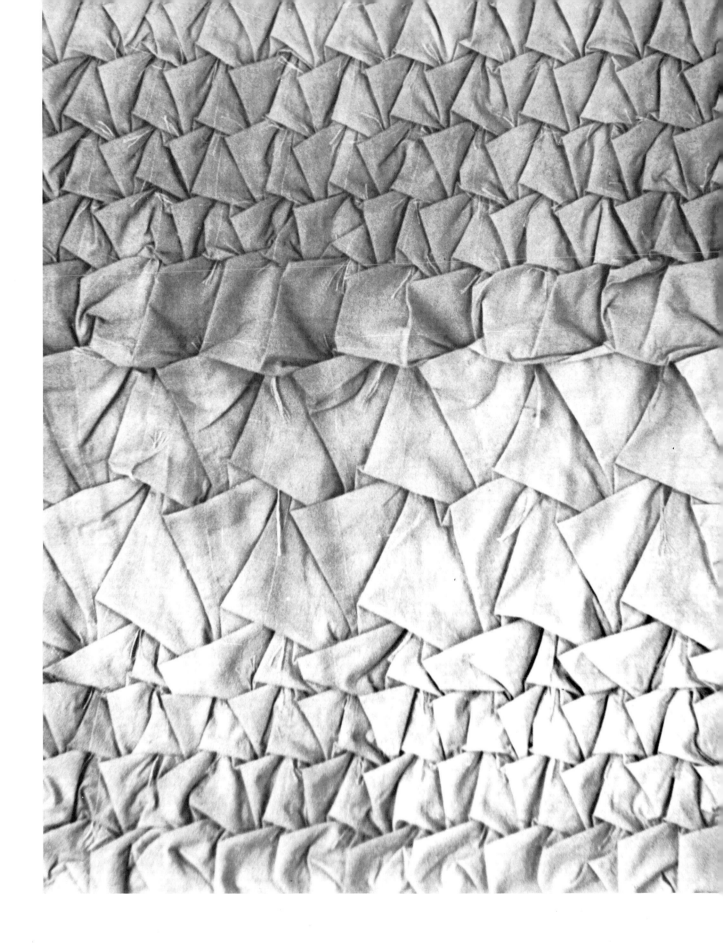

'Firefall' is the name of this textured work. The silk fabric is painted and then tightly pleated. This manipulated pleated material is applied to a large tubular framework. (In the collection of United Litho.)

Work: Ardi Davis
Photo: Bennett Davis

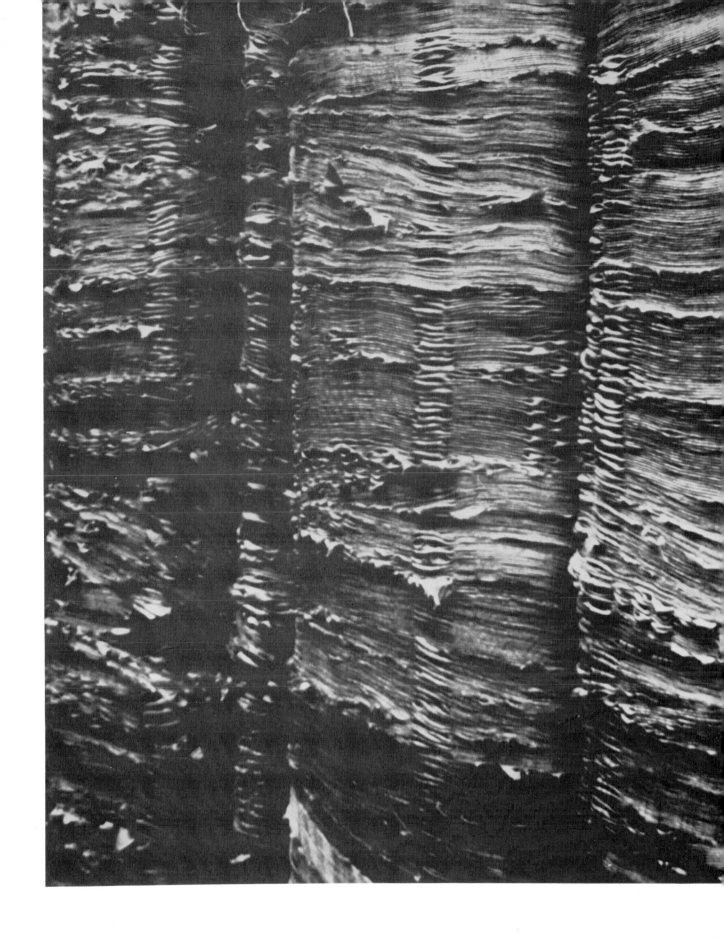

This vest made of grey linen, has insets of painted fabric in shades of pink, rose and dark grey . . . as well as bright red. See Techniques for shaped insets. The buttons are made using the scraps of the painted material, some are wrapped over silver cone shaped beads.

Photo: Maynard Smith

Work: Diane Ericson Frode

BUTTONS

Cut an elongated triangle of fabric (could also be leather or ultrasuede). Roll tightly and glue end in place. If fabric is used, waterproof the buttons with a liquid plastic (e.g. Varathane). Sew in place.

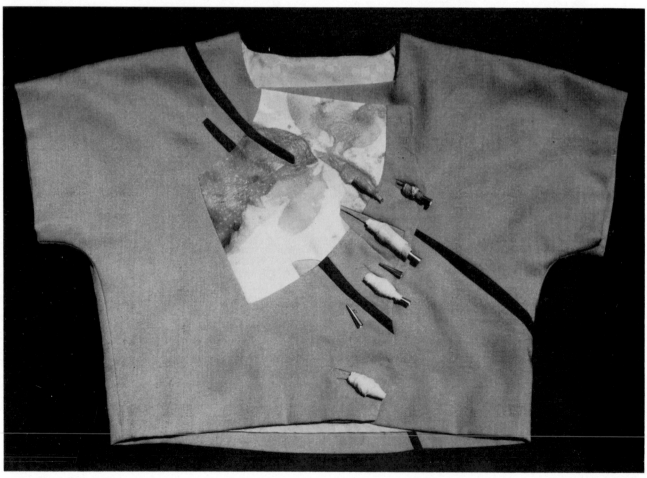

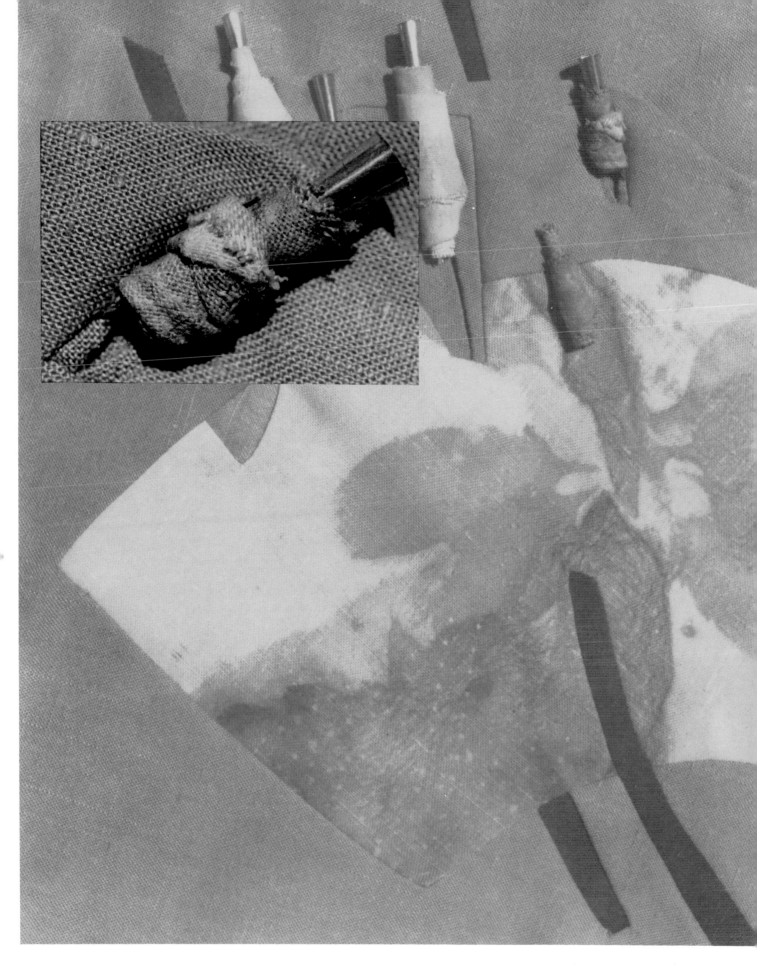

Four textures were created, using one fabric . . . very effectively. Large tucks were stitched and ironed to fold them over, these were then stitched in place. Pin tucks were sewn, this effect could also be achieved by stitching with a double needle and pulling on the bobbin thread to tighten the top stitching rows.

Double needle stitching over cotton crochet thread raised the seams. The twin needle was also used to make the grid pattern, by stitching in both directions. The various stitched pieces were cut up and sewn together for this pillow pictured below.

The double needle is fun to use. To achieve a shaded effect, try using two contrasting colors of thread, or two shades of the same color.

Photo & Work: Linda Kimura Rees

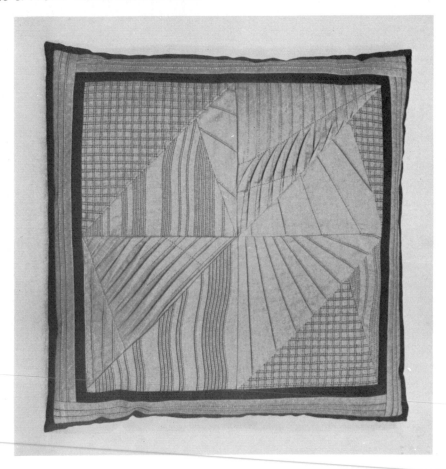

The 'product' that resulted from this manipulated fabric is a clutch bag. The plain cotton material was put through a pleater and drawn up very tight. This piece was placed on an underlining, then stitched through all layers by machine with a double needle using contrasting thread.

The remaining spaces were filled in with strips of ikat and other printed cloth to complete this eyecatching accessory.

Photo & Work: Karen Perrine

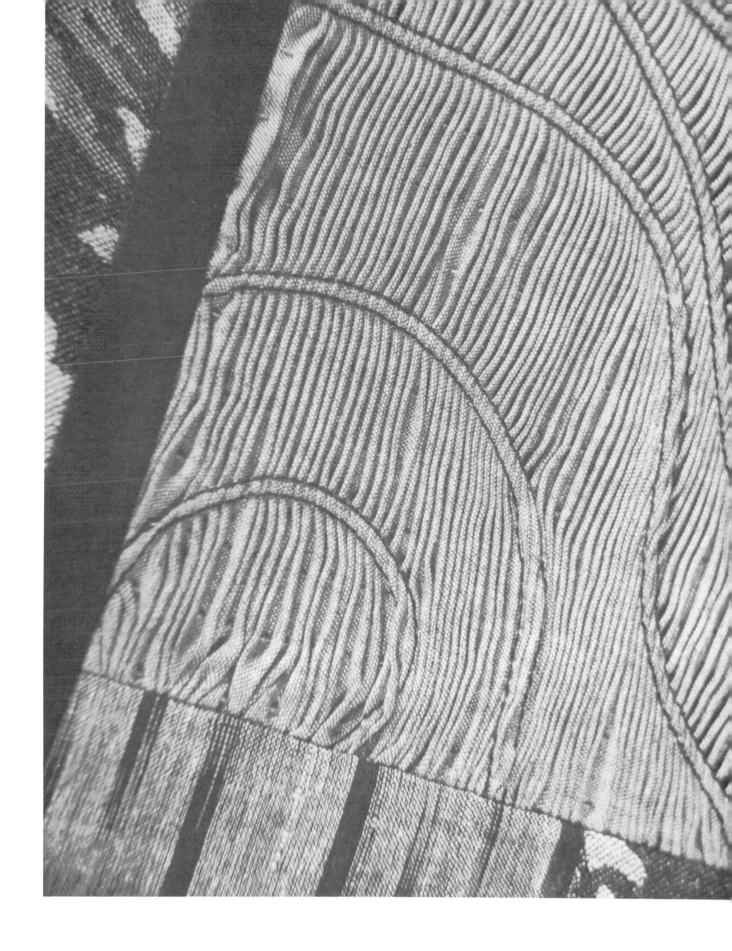

Oh! What a wonderful invention . . . the pleater!
Most of this piece is pleated on this great machine.
Except for the head, legs and tail . . all the fabric
whether it is painted or striped . . is pleated and
stitched to a muslin underlining. The top stitching
that holds the pleats in place is done with either a
double needle and 'regular' sewing thread or a large
(#18) needle and perle cotton.

The pads on the feet are stencilled using fabric paint.
The face is machine embroidered, French knot
whiskers and appliqued eyelids. . . . What a great
expression! By the way, this is George II, the first
being Karen Perrine's own cat. For information
about the time-saving pleater, see the supply list.
(In the collection of Lois Ericson , clones available)

Photo & Work : Karen Perrine

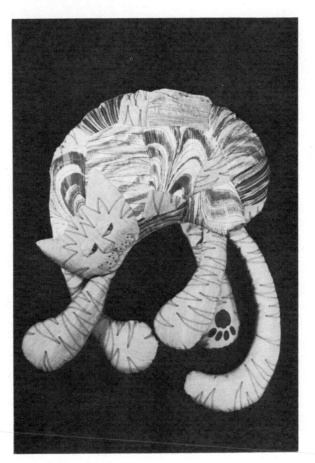

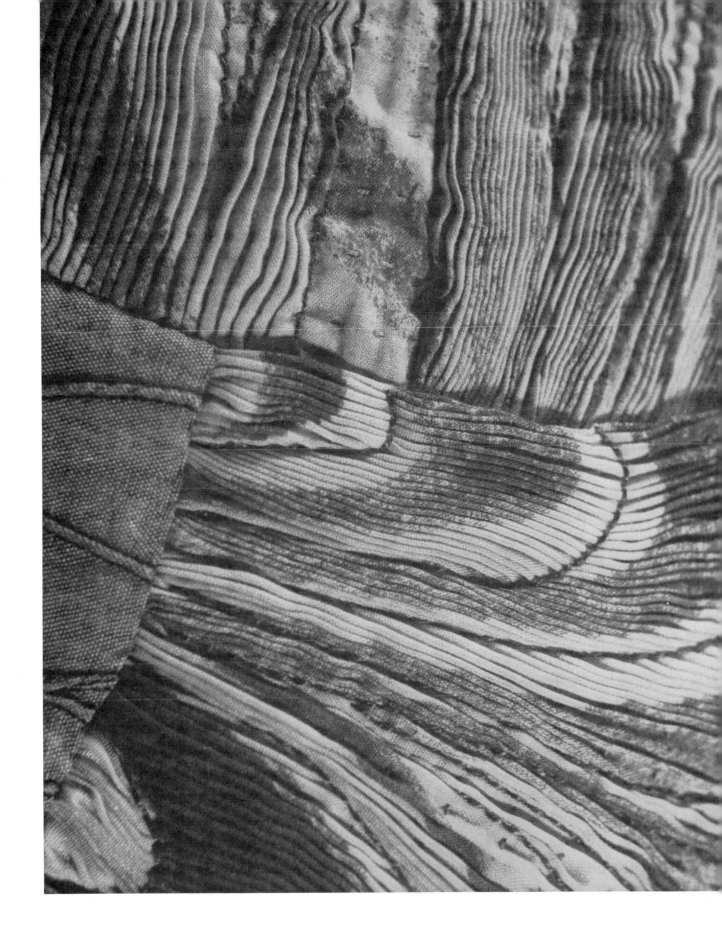

This quilt is called "View from Home". The view through the window is done with strip piecing using the fabric on the 'wrong' side. . . of course, we all know that there is no wrong or right side. There are seven angels stencilled and stitched on the snow. The trees are embroidered on. The popcorn is three dimensional, made with elastic thread in the bobbin of the machine. The fabric is put on an embroidery hoop--when you take it off the hoop, it puckers up. The leaves are cut double and stitched, then turned after cutting a small slit in the back of each.

Photo & Work: Lois Smith

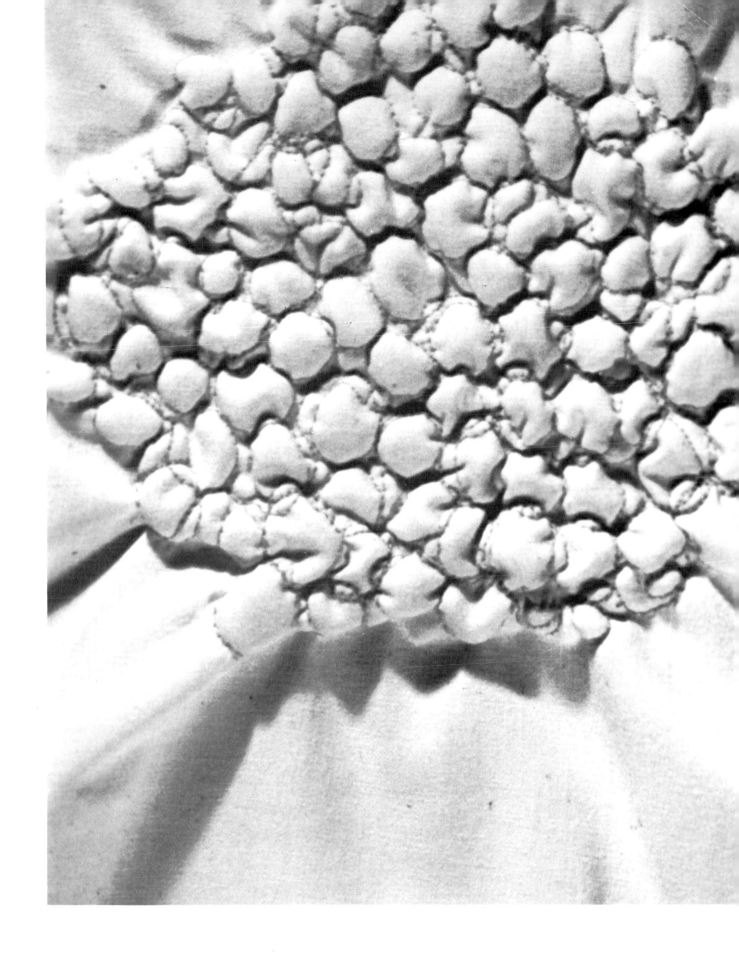

The name of this piece is "Kage Hinata" (meaning light and shadow). The techniques used on this 2 1/2" x 5 1/2" wall piece are pleating, tucking and twisting. The linen, silk and cotton fabrics are combined to create abstract 'paintings'. The fabrics are manipulated or flat with rows of stitching to add 'brush stroke' interest.

The colors are predominantly navy and pale blue with accents of lavendar, beige, turquoise and rose.
In the collection of Eda and Steven Baruch

Work: B.J. Adams
Photo: Breger & Assoc.

Half of this jacket is made of raspberry and dark red stripes (5/8") that are tucked and manipulated to show both colors in a wonderful pattern. The other half is made of dark red/grey very narrow stripe. These sections have been faced with dark red. Notice the striped insert that ties at the bottom edge and extends past the hem slightly.

The design on these overlapping sections started by covering a rip under the arm . . . and continued to include the pocket. The pocket on the tucked side of the jacket is in the side seam. A good example of how creative we can be when we don't have enough material . . . she said she used every little scrap of fabric.

Work: B.J. Adams

Simplicity . . in my classes I usually 'give' my students two words . . one is relationships and the other simplify. Both so important. It is easy to get caught up in all the possibilities for manipulating . . sometimes it's refreshing to simplify.

Liz Thoman has made piping of a subtle print. This would be a good way to use a painted fabric. . . maybe one that didn't turn out as we had hoped or pictured. These rows of piping, that are placed very close to each other, are stitched in place. This section became a pocket on a garment.

Photo & Work : Liz Thoman

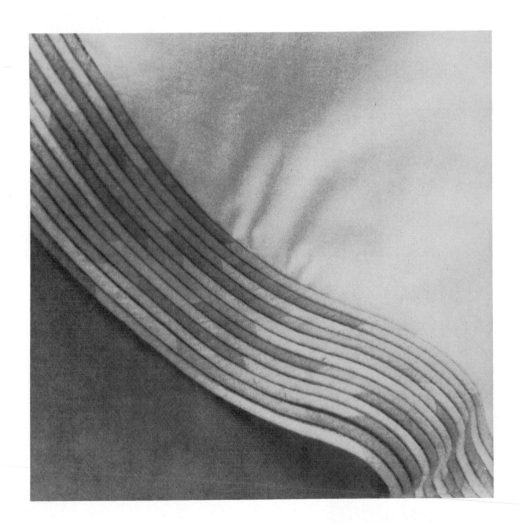

This piece is called "The Unemployment Line" . . . notice Ronald Reagan at the head of the line. The figurative pieces are created by drawing the idea in tissue paper. These are retraced and sewn onto the muslin. The result of this first step is a flat piece with figures sewn side by side. The backing is sewn onto the front of the figures, right sides together. The backs of each figure are slit from the back and stuffed. When each figure is stuffed, the entire unit is turned right side out and a wire armature is inserted.

Photo & Work : Caty Carlin

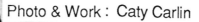

The focus of this piece was to work with the interplay of layers and colors. The textures were built up using an overcast foot on the sewing machine. A similar effect can be made by satin stitching over 20 cm double point knitting needles.

Work: Pat Rodgers

The name for this piece is "The Rocks that Wouldn't Stay Grey". The idea started with some lichen and moss covered rocks. . . to capture the effect of islands of plant growth was the objective. Bright colors, e.g., blue and orange kept sneaking into the piece. The techniques used are piecing, applique and quilting.

Photo : James Smeltzer
Work : Nancy Smeltzer

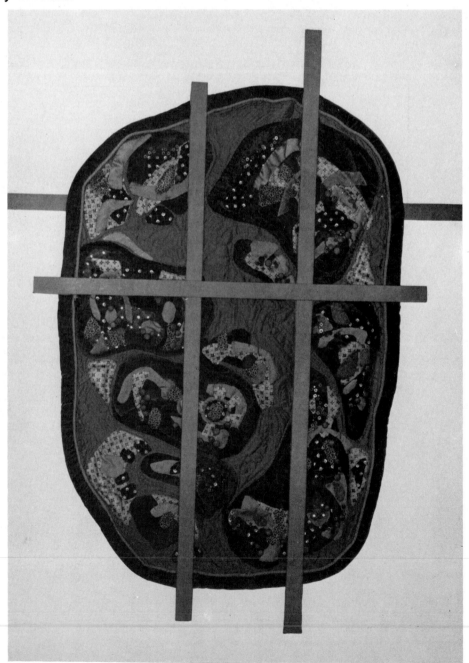

The film "The Purple Rose of Cairo" was the inspiration and ultimately the title of the piece, as well. Nancy just happened to have a purple fabric with black roses on it, so that started it all. Constructing a quilt around this one piece of material seemed like the next step. Her intention was to show a pharoah's exotic garden with columns and purple roses. The columns are made of a tapestry fabric with cotton moire for the water. Closely done quilting lines added to the effect of ripples. The beads are hand stitched around the edges of the flowers that are backed with buckram. In addition to the beading and quilting, much of this quilt is hand appliqued.

The fabrics are cotton, cotton/blends, gold lame.

I have known Nancy for several years, and I'm always surprised by each new piece of work. . . the images are very fantasy-like and the color range of her work is exciting.

Photo: James Smeltzer
Work: Nancy Smeltzer

The marbling technique came from the old bookbinding craft of decorating book end papers.

In brief, marbling ink or fabric paint is sprinkled over a thickened liquid and it 'floats' on top. The paint can be left . . . as is . . . or combed, stirred with a stick, blown about with a straw . . to create various patterns.

Fabric which has been treated with a mordant (if necessary) is then placed on top of the color which adheres to it. The fabric is then rinsed, dried, and ready for use. See technique section for detailed instructions.

After marbling this crinkled cotton in shades of peach and rose, the vest was hand quilted and embellished with ribbon and an appliqued bird.

Photos: Paul Dougherty
Work: JoAnne Dougherty

149

Boxes, cubes and stacked forms were the inspiration for this piece that is part of a series. Mop cord is the basic material . . short pieces are fastened together. These mop cord layers are stacked with waxed string in between. All are placed in wooden 'boxes' that are platforms with dowel corners.

Work: Mary Street

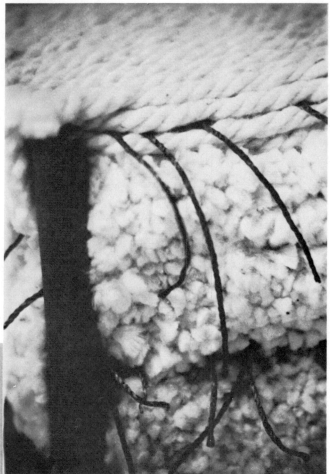

Machine embroidery is the technique used on this exquisite box made with Natesh thread. The stitching was done on a water soluble stabilizer*, that was attached to a wire framework. Remove the foot from the sewing machine, lower the feed dogs and set the stitch length on 0. Use a medium width zigzag and stitch around the wire ring. Baste the stabilizer to the ring and start stitching across, back and forth to create a web of stitching. This, of course, takes a little practice, but it is fun and a technique that can be applied to many projects.

On this little box, the top and bottom were completed, then a rectangle of fabric was also stitched on the stabilizer and attached to the bottom circle. The top has a 'hinge' and beads that were sewn on top to finish. *See Techniques

Work: Debbie Casteel

The Paper Coat is also one in the miniature coat series. These coats are constructed by wrapping strips of paper around a knitting needle. Foil and many textured papers are used, as well as firm silk fabrics. Some of the fibers are dyed and over-dyed for those special colors.

The colors and textures that are combined make the pieces seem jewel-like. Each one a treasure.

Photo & Work : Anne Syer

This piece is one of a series of miniature coats . . . . it is about 15" x 21" and called Feather Coat. It was made by fringing and layering strips of silk that had been dyed, using fiber-reactive dyes. Different silks take the dyes and fringe differently, which is fascinating.

In this constructed body of work, each piece is so exquisite. The pieces are usually placed in plexiglass boxes for display.

Photo & Work: Anne Syer

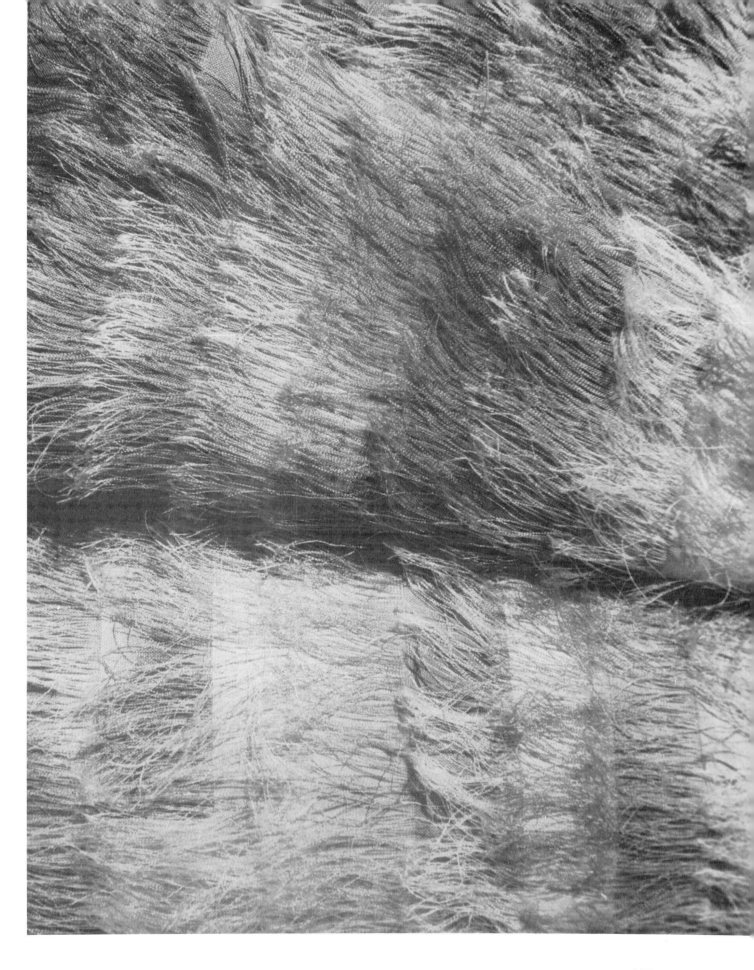

155

Papermaking is a centuries old art form that has been recently revived. It has become popular with many artists as the medium used to express their art.

After the pulp is made, Ingrid Evans forms the wet paper pulp into a particular shape and places it on screens or other flat surfaces. It is then left to dry completely. These pieces are sealed on both sides and painted. For additional support the paper is often mounted on canvas. The title is "Pictures at an Excavation"--one piece of a 16 unit series.

Photos & Work: Ingrid Evans

Handmade paper has become a very popular art medium. It is easy to learn the basic method.* It has many applications and possibilities for experimenting . . flat sheets, molded shapes, embossing, layering, combining with many other materials.

This book has wonderful deckle edges with embossed pages with threads and bits of fleece applied. *See Techniques for paper making.

Photo & Work : Barbi Racich

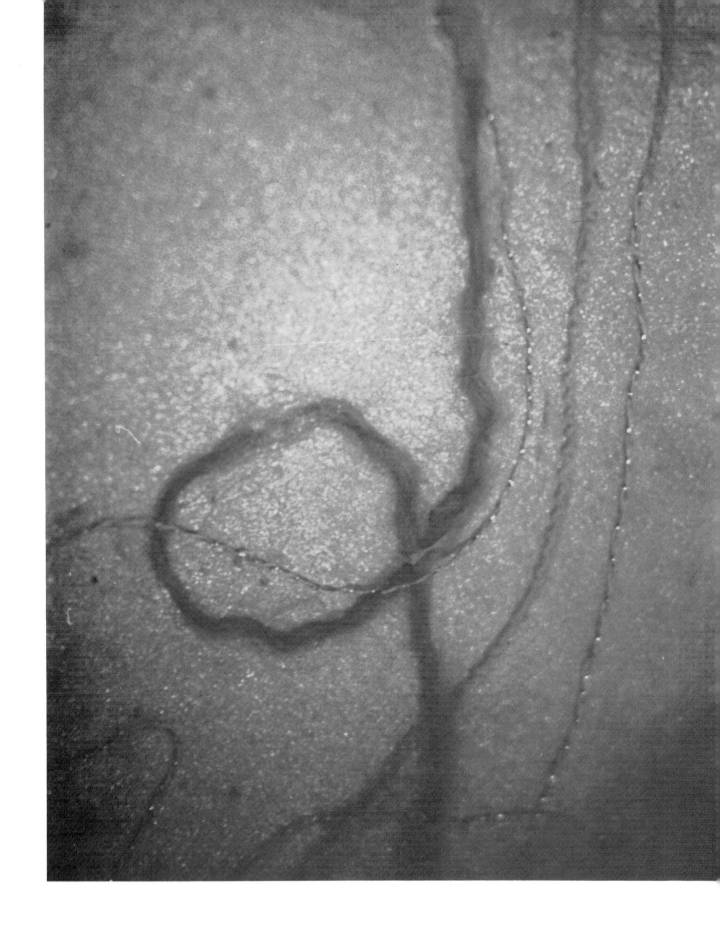

Feltmaking is an ancient art that has been practiced in many countries for centuries. The fleece is cleaned, carded and dyed, if desired. The 'sheets' of wool are placed between two layer of cheesecloth or other fabric and basted to keep it together. It is then wet with alternating hot and cold water and soap, rolled, pounded and kneaded until the fibers mesh together.*

In this piece the dark colored fleece is sandwiched between two light layers before processing. The felt is then cut into strips in the center and woven. The work is called "'Sky Piece". *See Techniques for felting.

Photo : John Echols
Work : Kathleen Curtis

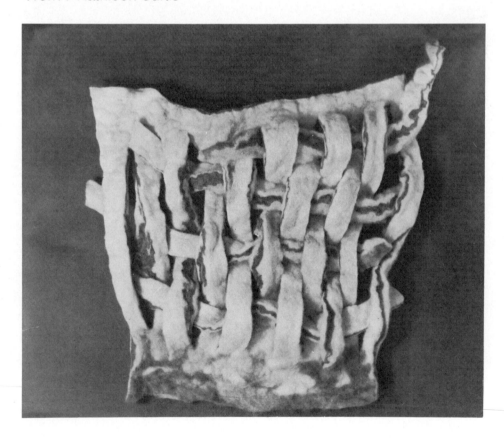

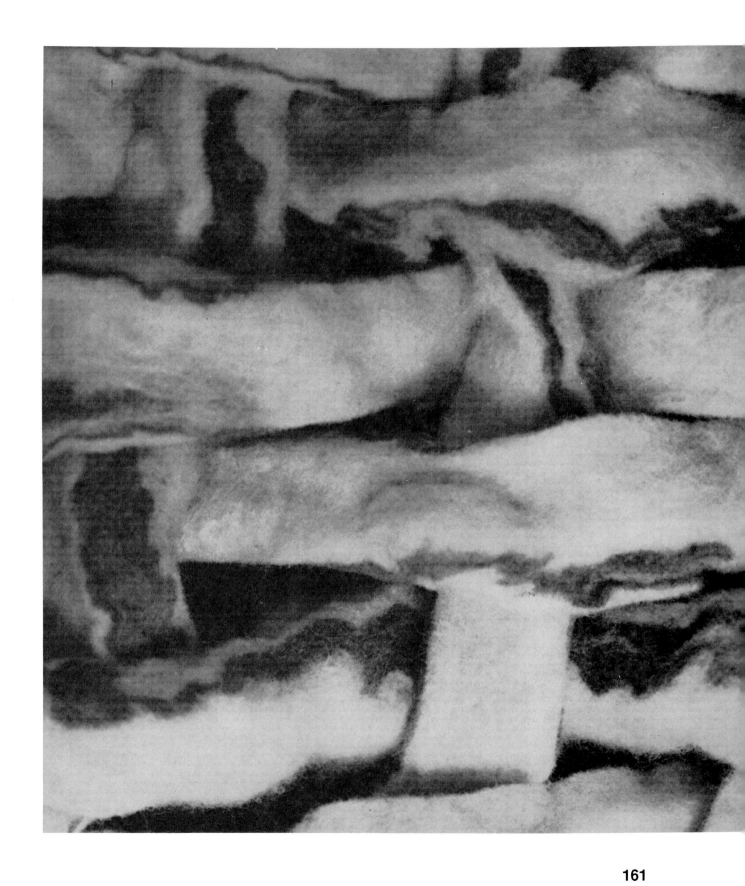

The aluminum wire is woven, cut and manipulated. Single elements are wired together to form a unit. The units are combined to create the form. This is just one piece in a sizable series... it is rare for this artist to do one single piece. Her work most often is part of an orderly sequence, her craftsmanship is superb.

Work: Gayle Luchessa

This work is called "Soft Drawings", one of a series. A mixed media process that combines paper, paint, and felt . . . all are held together by the wool fibers of the felting. Dimensional pieces are made separately and added to the whole during the felting process. Sizing is added as the last step to make it firm. Final shaping and forming is achieved while the work is air drying.

Photo & Work : Gayle Luchessa

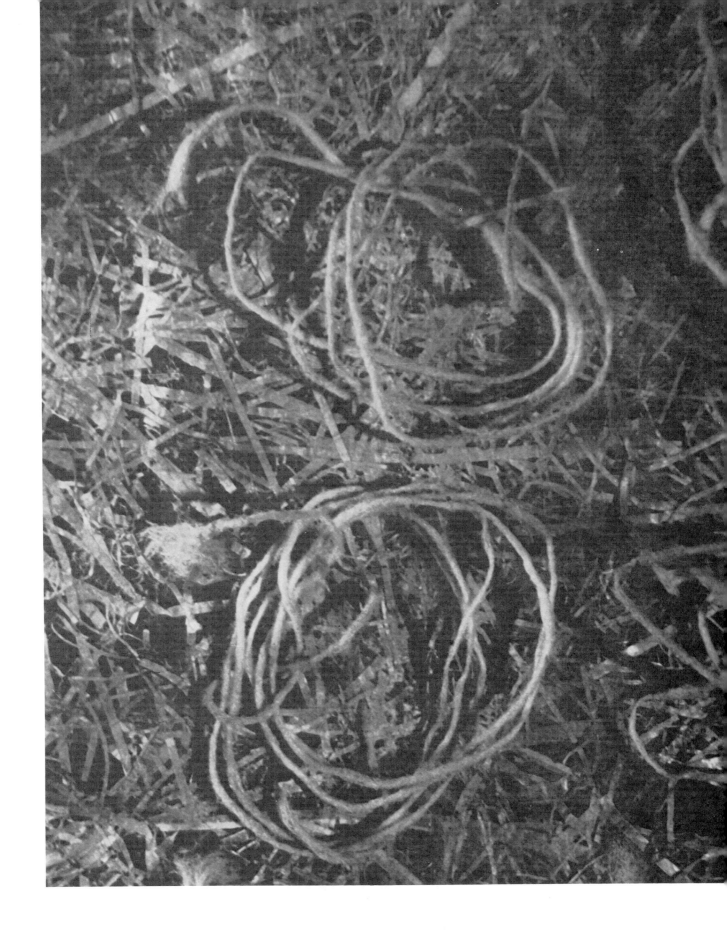

"Empty Garments" is the name of the series (14 pieces so far). It was started as a commentary on society women, who are pictured in fashion publications. Always jetting off to appear at some fancy event . . . the notation about the participants makes it seem that the garments are almost more important than the women . . . so why not just send the <u>dress</u>.

Texture and manipulating the fabric are part of making these 11" high pieces in various fabrics. They are stiffened and stand unaided . . as though someone has just stepped out.

Work: Author

Knits are a joy to work with, especially if one has a serger to finish the edges. The knit material is so supple and easy to manipulate. To create this texture, the applied knit piece is pulled one direction, folds and creases that result are stitched in place. Then the fabric is pulled in the opposite direction . . . folded and stitched. The applied piece was hemmed before it was attached. The fabric is an emerald green cotton/poly blend.

Work: Author

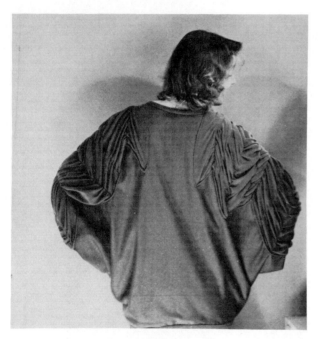

This silk jacket is pieced in shades of peach, mauve, pink, teal. The marbled fabric is turquoise, mauve, pink. The strip piecing is interspersed with stuffed tubes for additional texture. The piecing really emphasises the diagonal lines of this cocoon-like cut. The jacket is lined in the teal colored silk.

Marbled fabric: Jackson Brockette
Work: Author

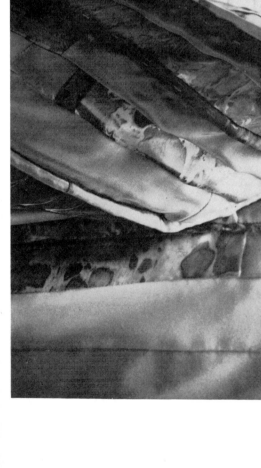

The challenge that I set up for myself on this project was to figure out how to change the direction of some tubes. Folding the tubes of material was one solution to create movement. I cut the underlining and sewed the shoulder seams together. The turned tubes of material were pinned and stitched in place . . folding where needed. The stitching lines could be more evident by using a satin stitch or double needle, if desired. The tubes are left loose in the back.

Another solution for this same challenge was to tie a single overhand knot in the fabric tubes, see photo below, right.

Work: Author

170

Stitching tucks in a fabric is a great way to create a texture. This jacket is made of cotton in stripes that are about 1 1/4" wide for the main part, the stripes on the sleeves are twice that width. The wooden buttons are from the Art Deco era. The "buttonholes" are covered cording that is handstitched to the finished edge, leaving spaces the appropriate size for the buttons.

Work: Author

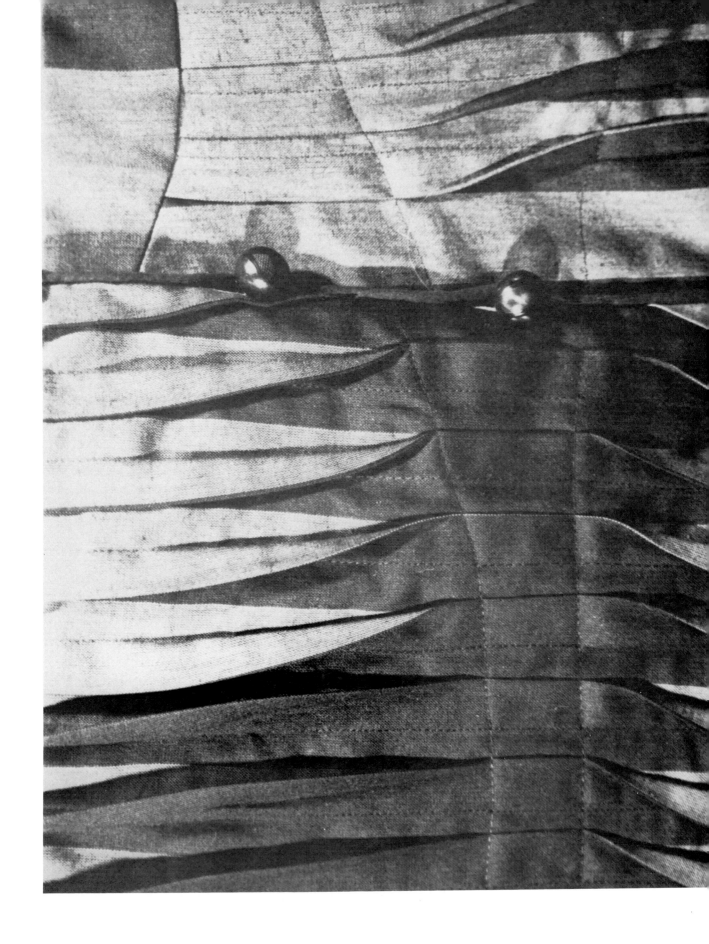

173

This woven jacket is made of a striped cotton/poly blend in jewel tones of fushia, teal and black. The main pattern pieces were cut from an underlining material, a densely woven cotton/linen. The five yards of the striped fabric were cut, lengthwise into 5" strips, and all the edges serged. Some strips were then attached at the shoulders forming the vertical lines for the weaving. As the horizontal strips were woven across, all the strips were pushed together . . . the folds and gathers appearing at random.

Work: Author

This box is made of interfacing -- <u>handwoven cotton and silk</u> -- that was inside some Japanese obis that were taken apart. Most of the applied design were the ravelings from the interfacing, the rest was chenille knitting yarn.

After the channels for the cord that holds the box together were stitched -- plastic drinking straws were inserted so the cording would be easy to insert.

Work: Author

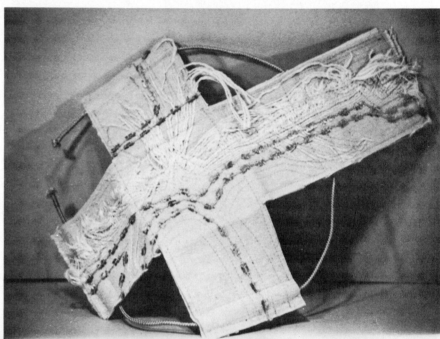

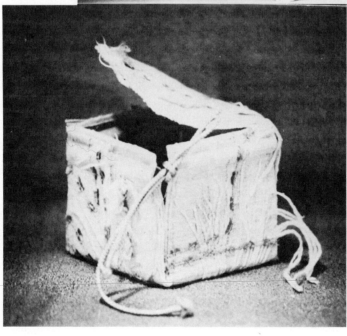

Since texture has become so important in my work, I have had a renewed interest in making wall pieces the 'product'. This group is called "Windows in Shades of Grey'. The sections are mounted on a padded wood surface. The window shades are manipulated tucks made of striped cotton. The ties fasten to flat horn bracelets.

Work: Author

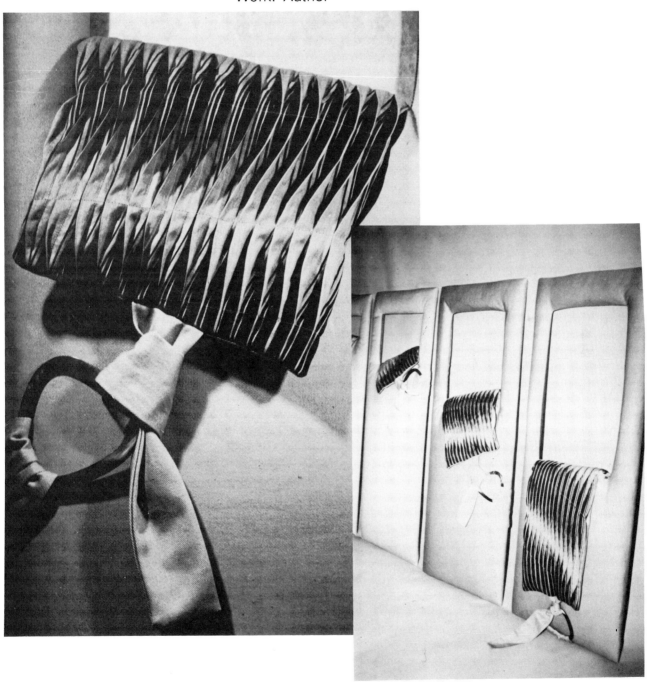

Experimenting is the key to unusual, inventive work ....trying out new ideas and combinations of techniques . . with no thought in mind of producing SOMETHING. Simply give yourself permission to play.

The awareness of the surface, shape, and line that we see affects the outcome and originality of our work. Seeing -- as opposed to looking -- is a skill to be learned. Refining this skill is a very important step in the process of expanding our creativity. We can also broaden our horizons by learning new techniques to add to our repertoire of skills already known . . maybe just looking at them with new vigor and enthusiasm.

An exciting thought to contemplate: we have talents that <u>we</u> don't even know about yet.

The samples in the technique chapter are the author's work.

technique

—from raw materials
. . . to texture

WRINKLED/STITCHED

Wrinkled fabric, often a source of irritation can be changed to an innovative design element. Natural fibers . . . silk, cotton, linen . . . are the best choices because they naturally wrinkle. The amount of fabric needed depends on how much of a wrinkled effect you want. In general, wrinkling the fabric vertically on the lengthwise grain usually takes up about 1/3 of the width. All over wrinkles that are stitched in all directions can take up as much as 1/2 the fabric in both directions. Plan your yardage accordingly.

Slightly dampen the fabric. Gather, pleat or crumple the material in your hands and tie to keep in place. Dry in dryer or air dry. On occasion, I have just piled the fabric on the ironing board and ironed the wrinkles in.

Next, cut a piece of underlining fabric several inches larger than the length and width of the pattern pieces. If you don't mind it being a little stiff, Stitch Witchery may be placed between the underlining and the wrinkled fabric to secure while stitching.

Pin the wrinkled fabric to the underlining, pinning as needed to establish the pattern you will stitch. You may wish to baste instead of pinning or fusing.

Machine stitch along the wrinkles. Stitch as much or as little as you wish, letting the stitching outline the shapes of the wrinkles. There are numerous ways of varying this basic technique for different effects. Try stitching with threads in a contrasting rather than matching color. Or use a double needle with threads in two nearly matching shades. Corded piping may be added where the wrinkles are large enough to cover the raw edges.

When you finish stitching, cut out your garment. This technique takes a lot of thread and is time consuming . . but well worth the effort.

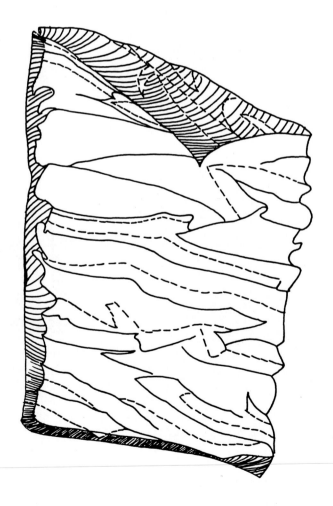

PIECING

Piecing is a method of putting sections of fabric together . . . might also be called patchwork or strip patchwork. The word 'piecing' seems to encompass many related techniques.

Method:
Cut out the lining fabric. If it is to be quilted, baste the batting to the lining. Cut the strips for the patchwork, whatever width you choose . . . 1" to 3" . . . the wider the strips, the faster the project. Whole strips can be used or you may wish to piece them, with a definite design in mind.

Sew the pieces together to make the strips, if you are piecing them, press seams open. If you make the decisions on several strips at a time, you can sew and press more than one. It seems to save a little time.

Start at one side or in the middle of the lining piece (front or back). Pin the first strip down on top of the lining (with or without the batting). Take the next sewn strip, place it right side down on top of the first strip. Stitch in place, make sure the piece underneath is included in the seam . . . it is impossible to fix neatly if it is not remedied immediately. Keep piecing, pressing, and stitching until you've covered the lining. Each succeeding piece of fabric covers the raw edge of the previous piece, so there is basically no handwork.

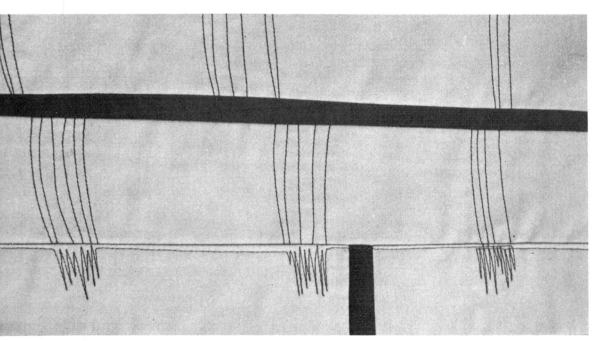

STITCHING

Machine stitching is one of the easiest ways for designing unusual fabrics. The most obvious is topstitching . . . try using a double or triple needle with various shades of threads.

Try using an overcast foot if there is one made for your machine, not as an edging but as a satin stitch in various widths. Be careful not to touch the foot as you decide the width of the stitches. The stitch length would be 0.

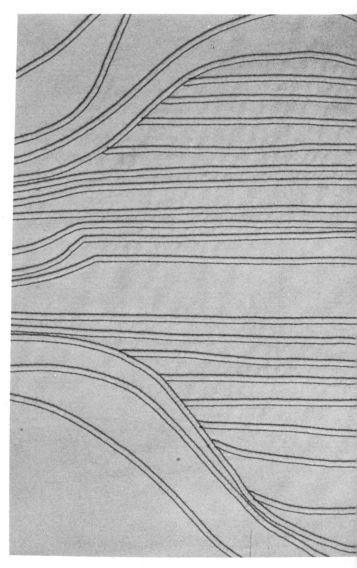

Padding the fabric to be stitched can give a design some added interest and give extra body to the material. Multiple rows of stitching when combined with batting can really make a fabric stiff, if for instance you were stitching a box or belt or purse.

To stitch with unusual threads, i.e. metallic, boucle or any other threads difficult to thread through the sewing machine needle, hand wind onto the bobbin. Stitch on the wrong side of the fabric.

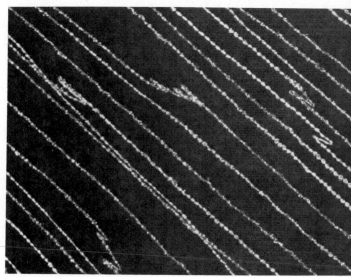

184

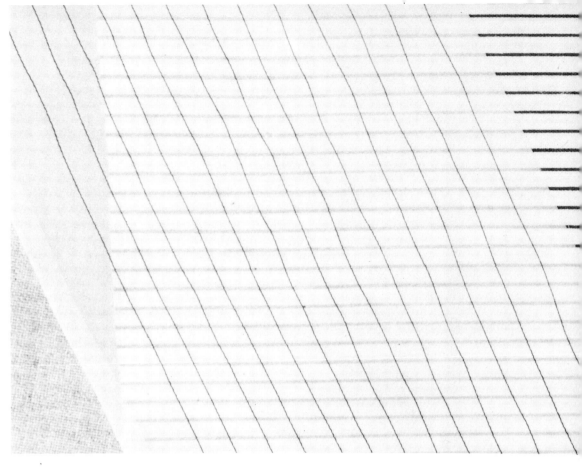

Stitching on sheers and overlaying on top of another
print or stripe will give some dimension. The sheers
can be organza, voile, or batiste or ?

To achieve a linear effect, try couching interesting
yarns or strings using the zigzag stitch (narrow) on
the sewing machine. If the thread is a good match or
if you use an invisible nylon thread, the utilitarian
zigzag stitch slips by unnoticed.

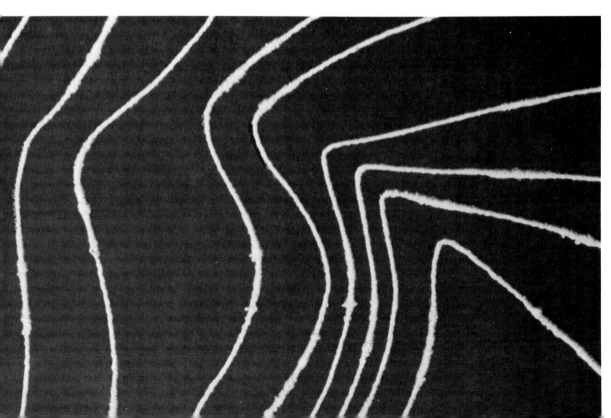

TUCKS

Most of the tucks I've made and manipulated have been stripes because I like the movement that occurs with stripes, especially on garments. Another reason for choosing stripes is that there are lines to follow as you stitch the tucks.

It is easiest to do this technique if the width of the stripes you choose is 3 to 1 in ratio. If the stripes are even in size, especially 1/4" to 1/2" in width, the tucks are so close together that it is really time consuming.

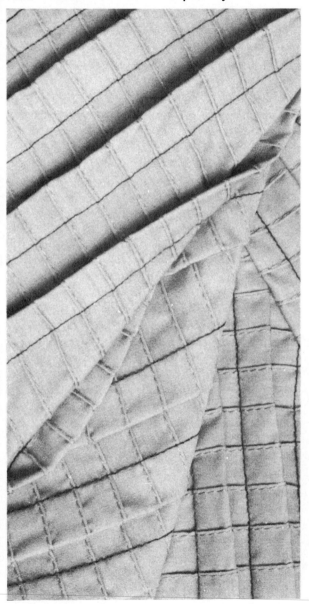

I cut the fabric the length needed, and then start stitching the tucks, using the vertical stripes as my guide. When the piece is finished, I press the tucks from one end with all one color showing. Stitch across the tucks to keep them in that direction. I press the next section so the other color shows, then stitch. Continue until piece is all pressed and stitched. . . then I cut out the pattern pieces, if the tucked fabric is to be a garment.

When using the manipulated tucked fabric, consider circles, squares and triangle (or other shapes) when stitching to keep the tucks in place.

If the material to be pleated is plain or printed, other than a stripe, the effect is more subtle but the texture is apparent, the result is eyecatching. It isn't vital, to me, if the tucks are the same width or distance apart, so I don't measure, I make a crease and stitch the tucks in place. Be easy on your self, it probably will be more interesting anyway if the rows aren't 'perfect'.

The light piece on the left is first stitched using a pin tucking foot on the sewing machine, then larger tucks have been made in different directions.

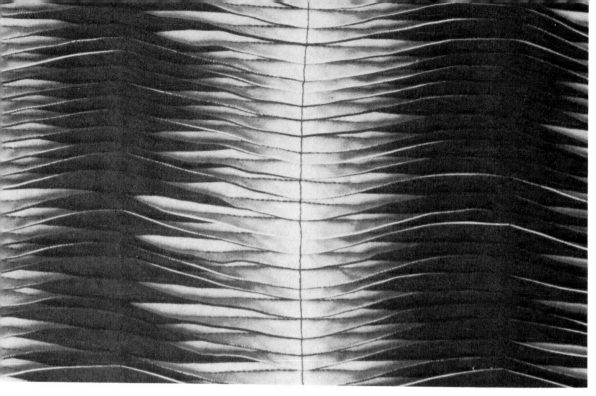

The tucks have been stitched in the bold evenly striped cotton, above, then pressed in the appropriate direction. The vertical stitching, very apparent on the white with the black thread, holds the tucks in place.

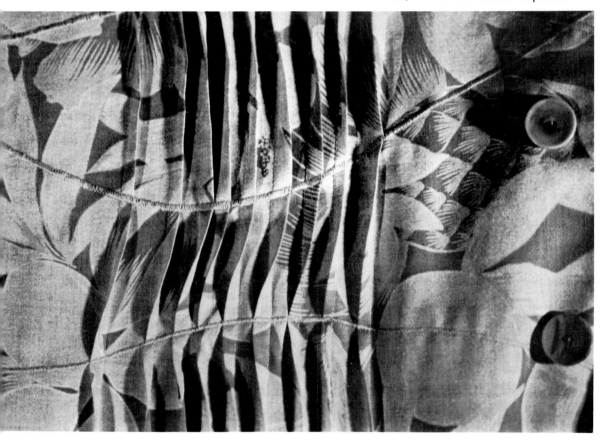

tucking a subtle print

CORDING

Method:

1. Cut bias strips generously to 'go around' the cording you've chosen. Remember it is easier to trim it later.

2. Measure the length of bias from one end of the cording. No .. . don't cut it! Now pin your bias, wrong side out, to the second length of cording.

3. Using a zipper foot, stitch across the cording and bias, then stitch along the cording all the way down the side. Be careful not to catch the cording in the stitching.

4. Trim close to the stitching.

5. Draw the cording out of the bias.

6. Voila .. it's covering the first length of cording. Now when you cut it off, the remainder of the cording will be all one piece.

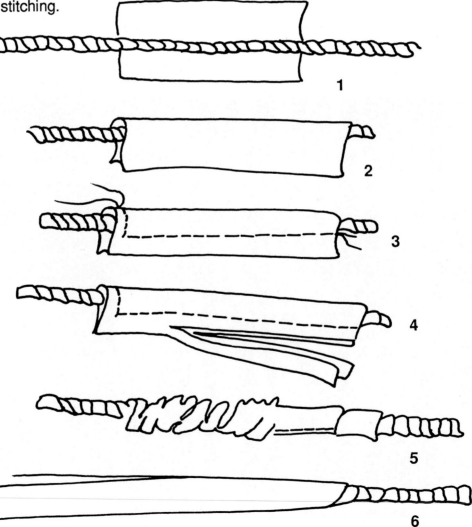

1. Cut the strips of bias at least four times the width of the cord to be covered. It is much easier to handle a wider strip, even if you waste some.

2. Fold it over the cording, right side out.

3. Using a zipper foot, stitch close to the cord, using a basting stitch.

To add interest to your piping, strips of fabric or ribbon can be applied, see diagram 4. To apply . . . if using fabric strips, the edges should be pressed under but not sewn. Fold ribbon or fabric strips over the bias piping. Pin in place and stitch as you are making the piping.

To apply piping to the garment: pin the cording to the edge of the fabric at the seam allowance and stitch using the zipper foot. Stitch from the bias side, so you can use the other stitching line as a guide. Place the companion pieces of the garment together. Pin in place, right sides together. Stitch through all thicknesses, using the previous stitching as a guide.

Note: Using the stitching lines as a guide assures an even professional look. Also clip the curves and corners, where it is needed, as you would any other seam.

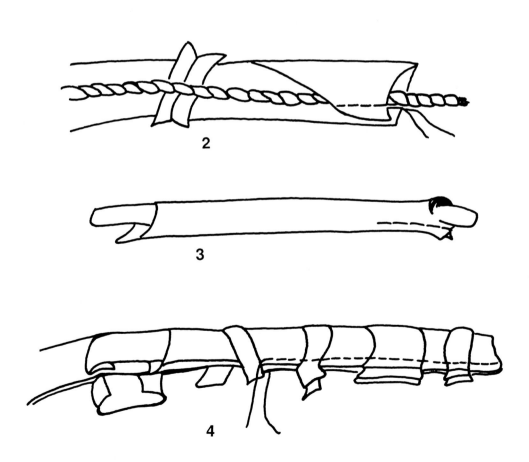

2

3

4

FACED SHAPES

To use very intricate shapes in your work with little or no handwork, you may wish to consider using facings on the finished edges.

Cut facings or bias strips for the edges to be finished, in the same or contrasting material. If a bias strip is used, the edges of the entire shape can be finished, if desired. Simply stitch the 1 1/2" (or wider) bias strip to the edge to be finished.

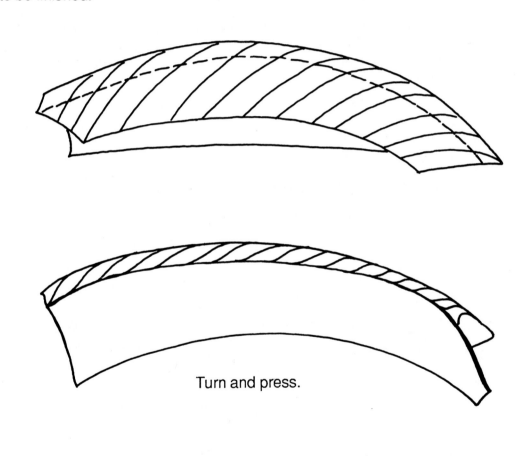

Turn and press.

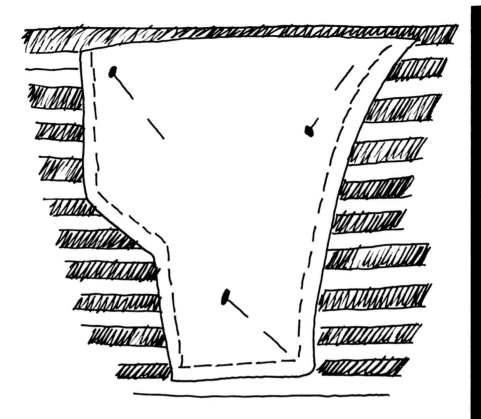

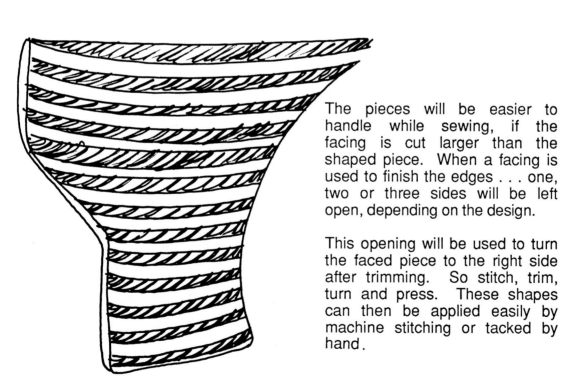

The pieces will be easier to handle while sewing, if the facing is cut larger than the shaped piece. When a facing is used to finish the edges . . . one, two or three sides will be left open, depending on the design.

This opening will be used to turn the faced piece to the right side after trimming. So stitch, trim, turn and press. These shapes can then be applied easily by machine stitching or tacked by hand.

191

Some examples of faced shapes

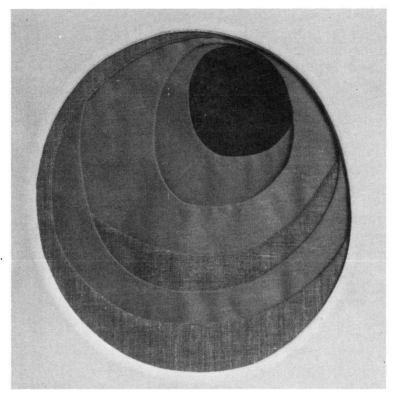

These faced circular shapes would be a great pocket idea.

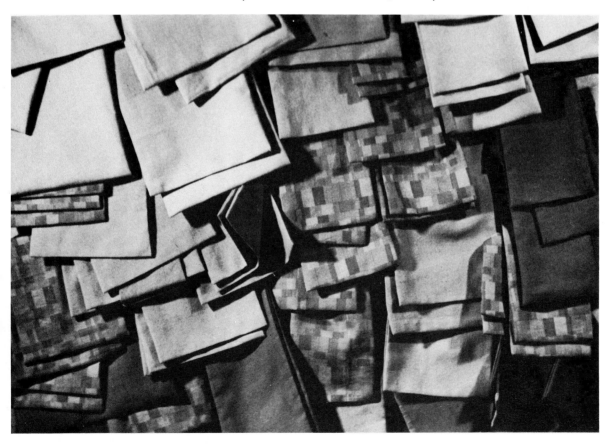

SHAPED INSETS

The technique of shaped insets gives us an unusual opportunity to insert color where needed or desired. The insets can be emphasized by using piping in the seams, gradual shading or including pieces of already textured fabric.

1. Draw the desired shape on the wrong side of the fabric. This first line is the finished seam line. Draw the second line to the inside of that first line (seam allowance) which will be the cutting line. Next, cut the piece to be inset, adding an equal seam allowance. Clip all curves, mark the point with a thread or pen.

2. Pin and stitch one side, don't stretch the seams. Grade seams. Press this first seam flat either in or out depending on the finish you want.

3. Working from the front side of your piece, turn the seam allowance under. Lift and pin seamline along other side of inset.

4. Fold back so you can stitch on the seamline. Sew from the point out, being careful not to stretch. Note: always maintain grainlines.

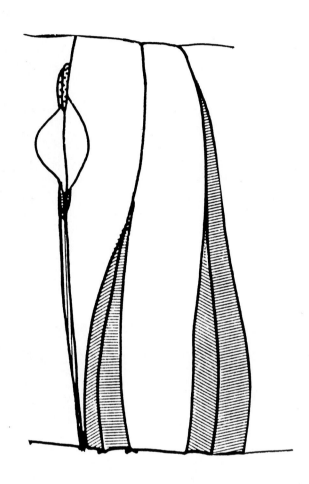

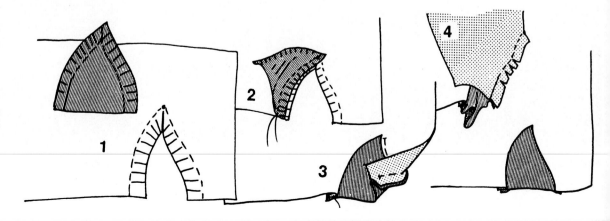

SHIRRING

Shirring is a method of gathering using a long basting stitch, usually in some kind of pattern. Simply machine stitch the design on the fabric and draw up to gather as much as desired. Nearly any shapes work well and it is surprising how different the material looks afterwards. Where the spaces are rounded, you may wish to pad them with a little batting.

If the stitching lines need emphasis, covered cording is a good solution. Tack rows of the covered cording on top of the gathering lines.

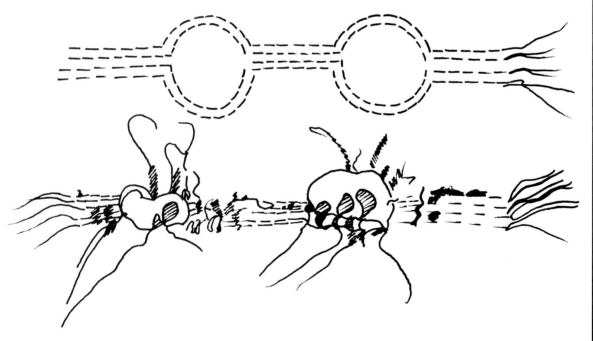

SMOCKING

I call my pieces -- nearly smocked -- because I only pleat my fabric and stitch it to the backing. There is no embroidery involved in this contemporary treatment of the material. The use of a pleater simplifies the procedure and makes it fun, instead of tedious.

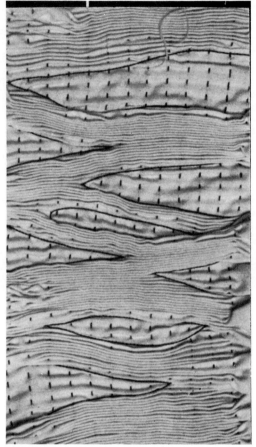

I pleat the fabric, using a double thread, on the pleater. I next arrange the pleats and place this fabric on an underlining. Stitch through all thicknesses on the machine to hold in place. I leave the "gathering" threads in. Word of caution...soft, light, thin fabrics work best with the pleater. See Suppliers for pleaters.

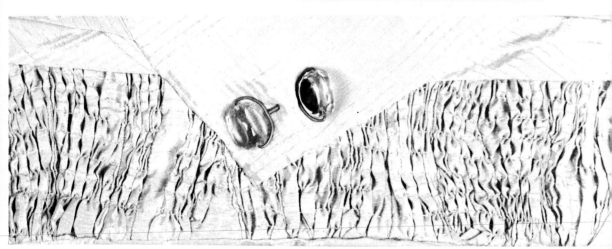

If you don't have a pleater and/or would like to try some other smocking/shirring techniques, here are a few suggestions.

Mark the dots on your fabric, if you use a checkered material it makes it really easy . . . just use the squares as you would the dots. Pick up the corners of the

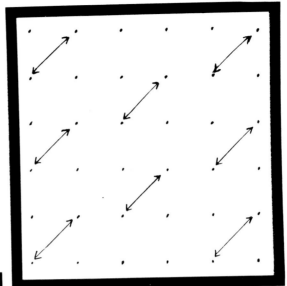

squares from the wrong side of the fabric, pin as the arrows indicate. Using a zigzag stitch, stitch length on 0, fasten to hold together, or sew by hand if you wish. Try using this technique with a variety of fabrics for some unusual results.

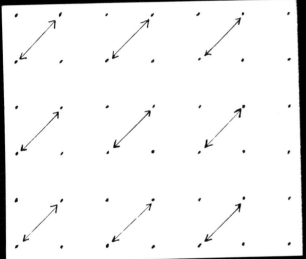

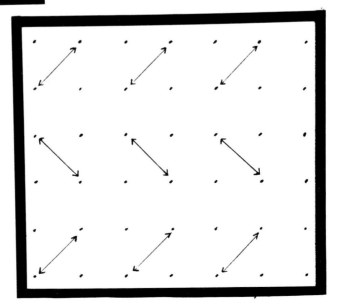

TUBES

There are a variety of ways to use tubes of fabric. They can be: woven . . combining several widths, colors, or textures placed side by side and stitched to a backing. Sheer tubes may be stuffed with yarns or small scraps of cloth. Tubes may also be the solution for keeping pleats in place, possibly placed at various angles. And then, of course, for the usual --button-loops, ties, straps, applique.

Cut the strips three times wider than the finished tube. If you want long pieces, stitch several cut strips together. Then fold in half and stitch, as shown. Note: if the fabric is thick or has a nap, long pieces may be difficult to turn.

No need to trim the seams. Make an indentation at the end that has been stitched closed. Put the turning tool (see below) in that depression. Slide the fabric tube onto the tool. Cut off the very end, the one that was stitched. Press strips with the lengthwise seam in the middle of the back of the strip.

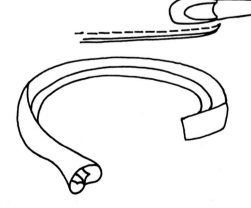

It is very easy to turn the tubes if you have some kind of a long smooth tool for that purpose. Alternatives to making a tool could be a chopstick or a knitting needle (use the blunt end).

To make a tool, you will need a 15"-20" piece of #9 galvanized wire. Flatten both ends with a hammer. Smooth rough places with a grinder or coarse sand paper. It's ready to use.

TUBES, continued

Note: If the back of the tube isn't going to show, fold with wrong sides together and stitch along the long side and press with the seam in the middle of the back . . . don't turn. No one will see the cut edges.

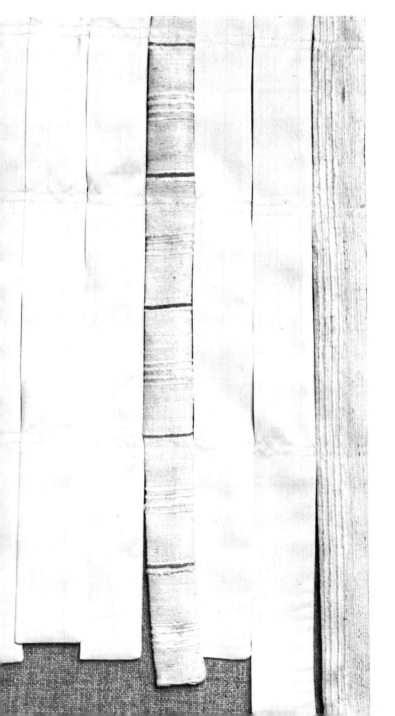

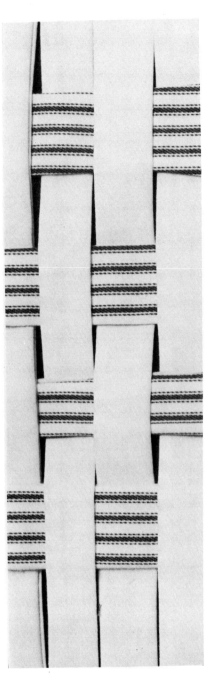

These turned tubes, starting with the black strips are placed diagonally on top of a pin striped background. The white strips are placed on top of the black ones. The medium colored strips are then woven across. This pattern was inspired by a quilting pattern.

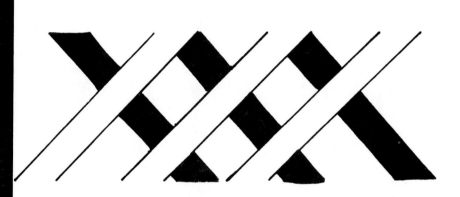

200

WATER SOLUBLE STABILIZER

(trade names . . . Solvy, Aqua-solv, Stitch 'n spray . . .)

How to use:
Draw or trace design on the 'pebbled' side of the stabilizer, with a soluble ink marker . . . several people recommended using Deco Permanent Paint Marker (it comes in colors, so use one that is easy to see).

Keep hands dry (remember it dissolves), and store unused portion in ziplock bag to keep it crisp.

For knits, terrycloth, fabrics with a nap:

Place a single layer of the stabilizer on top of the fabric. Using a hoop, frame as usual and do your stitching. After the embroidering is complete, tear away the stabilizer outside the design. Spray some water on the stabilizer to dissolve it inside the design. Dry fabric. (Place between pieces of fabric and iron, for instance, or use dryer.)

For standard cottons, cotton-poly blends and other woven fabrics:

Place single layer of stabilizer underneath fabric. Using a hoop, frame as usual and do your stitching. After embroidery is complete, remove stabilizer around outside of design. Spray water on stabilizer, or place in a dish or pan containing water and immerse stabilizer for about 2 minutes. When removing the stabilizer spray the piece "just a little" if it is not something which is going to be worn. To say that the piece can become "crisp" is an understatement. If you want a project to be stiff, then use only as much water as you HAVE to and dry it right away with an iron or blow dryer.

MARBLING

The technique for marbling utilizes a product called "Marbled Dust" (see Suppliers). It is easy to use and the results are very good.

Mix 1 Tbsp. 'Dust' in 1 1/2 qts. hot tap water and stir until dissolved. Cool.

Make a solution of alum (buy at drug store) . . . 2 Tbsp. alum to 1 pt. warm water. Dip fabric or brush paper with alum mixture. Prepare several pieces at a time and stack to keep damp.

Liquitex acrylic paint is suggested, but I've tried other fabric paints with success. Dilute with water to the consistency of thin cream.

Pour the marble dust mixture (you may wish to double or triple the batch in recipe above) in a large flat pan. Drip, spatter or dribble paint carefully on top of the marble dust mixture. Now the design can be made by combing, lightly stirring with a toothpick or chopstick, blowing with a straw or ??

Slowly lower the damp fabric or paper on top of paint. The paint will stick to the surface. Rinse in clean water, to dry place on newspapers.

Suggestion: Try using scraps of leather or ultra suede for beautiful results.

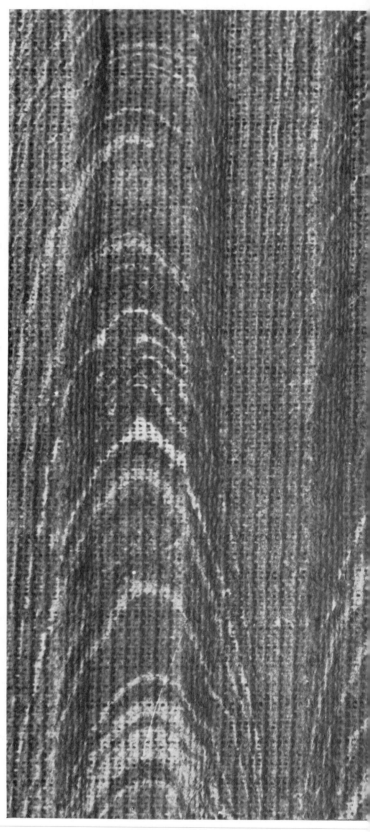

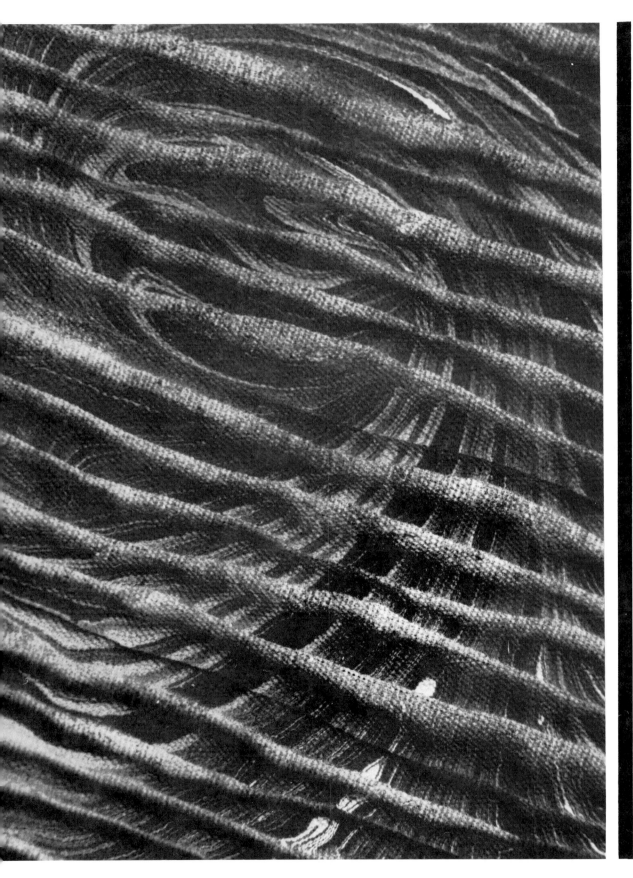

These close-ups show the marbling on commercially
pleated/crinkled cotton by Joanne Dougherty.

PAPERMAKING

This is a very sketchy explanation of this technique. If you are at all intrigued, you will want to get a book on the subject.

Start with about a cup of torn, soaked paper and add cut up plant matter. Pre-soaked cotton linters could also be used, about 1/4 cup at a time.

Put the fibers in a blender, nearly filled with water. Blend, making sure the motor on the blender isn't straining....the mixture may not be thin enough.

Color can be added in the blender, if desired. Different things to try would be food coloring, dyes from others papers, i.e. tissue or construction papers, fabric dyes, or natural additives like coffee or tea.

The blender mixture is now poured into a large vat or tub of water, to be collected on a screen or fine mesh that is in a frame or hoop. After the screen has been dipped and the mixture collected, the newly formed sheet will be transferred to a piece of felt, or other heavy cloth. Several layers with felt in between each layer may be stacked on top of each other. The sheets can be air or heat dried.

Caution: do not pour water from your vat into sink drains because the remaining fibers could clog your drains.

See Suppliers list for materials and books, also bibliography for books on the subject.

FELTING

Materials:
Fiber: Clean wool tops, sliver, roving or batt
Fabric base: A large piece of tightly woven fabric (not wool)
Soap: Mild Liquid detergent in a squirt bottle (e.g., Ivory Liquid)
Water: a) 1 pot boiling water
b) 1 pot cold water
Other: Ladle, Plastic gloves
Optional: More fabric or nylon netting, needle & dryer

Procedure:
1. Lay out fabric base someplace that will not be harmed by lots of water and soap (e.g., laundry room, patio, deck, driveway).
2. Layer and criss-cross fiber pieces on the fabric base to a depth of 3-4".
3. Squirt on some liquid detergent.
4. Ladle on some boiling water.
5. Knead and rub fiber using a circular motion of the palms and fingertips. Use gloves if your hands are sensitive to heat.
6. Ladle on cold water and continue to knead and rub. You will feel the fibers "solidify" under your touch.
7. Repeat soap and hot and cold water treatments, and continue to knead the piece until it becomes a piece of SOFT FELT.
8. Once it begins to felt, a piece may also be rolled up in the fabric and beaten with a stick or stamped on with a foot.

Some variations:
1. To make a piece of HARD FELT, try some of the following:
a) Quilt fiber or soft felt between 2 pieces of fabric or nylon net. Run this quilted sandwich through the washer and dryer. (Hint: Use Hot Wash, Cold Rinse and Gentle Cycle in the washer; use the Gentle Cycle in the dryer.
b) Some additives that harden felt are vinegar, starch and glue.
2. Layer different colors of fiber; add odd bits of yarn, thread and tinsel.
3. Create pockets and flaps by placing small fabric pieces in between layers of fiber, thereby preventing the fiber layers from felting together in certain areas.
4. For 3-D forms, felt fiber over and around plastic bowls and bottles.
5. Felt items that have been woven, crocheted or knitted.

Experiments or ideas that lead to projects or a series of work have many starting points.

. . . From the idea of a specific finished product, i.e., a belt or jacket, the considerations would be centered around the purpose of the product.

. . . From someone else's direction, a problem to solve or a given direction to explore.

. . . From a technique, to be explored and experimented with, maybe changing the scale of it ... to become the focus.

. . . From the materials, consider shape that will give unity to the whole piece when combined with color and texture.

If, after all these examples and suggestions in this book, I have not helped to spark your creativity . . . maybe you need JUST a buzz word.

Fold	Collect	Shapes -Round
Crease	Cluster	Square
Bend	Knot	Cube
Wrinkle	Assemblage	Triangle
Pleat	Gather	Cone
Tuck	Join	Tube
Flute		Pointed
	Ravelling	Curved
Drape	Fray	
Wrap	Cut	Calligraphy
	Slash	Hieroglyphics
Twist	Slit	Characters
Distort	Rip	
Coil	Groove	Indent — Bundles
Spiral	Aperture	Gouge — Bind
Entwine		Furrow — Bale
Irregular	Layer	Imprint — Roll
Assymetrical	Laminate	Emboss
Turn	Cover	Ridges
	Coating	
Fasten		Grids
Hook	Perspective	Framework
Connect		Network
Unite	Pocket	Compartments
Adhere	Pouch	Mesh
	Container	
Compress		Pattern-Separate
Shrink	Reveal	and rearrange
Pucker	Veil	Reduce and enlarge
	Overlays	Repeated
	Overlapping	
206	shapes	Lines -Diagonal
	Sheers	Interrupted
		Various widths

artists

_____from coast
. . . to coast

Most of the people listed are professional artists, serious about their work (some not so serious). Many teach seminars and also sell their work, so their addresses are included if you'd like to connect with them directly.

I have asked them to write a few lines about how they feel about their work . . . I am so pleased to present them to you . . . and to thank them all for the time, talent and the creativity they have given so freely.

I am constantly looking for new ideas . . . new ways to develop a texture or design. I become bored repeating something already created . . . so I try to change it. Sometimes this is difficult, sometimes . . . easy. Ideas usually do not make great leaps but rather are chained together. . . as gradual changes occur. Other times there will be a leap to an unconnected idea . . that is fun! Ideas do come faster than the time to try them . . Oh! for unlimited time.

B.J. Adams
2821 Arizona Terr. NW
Washington, D.C. 20016

I love everything about working with fibers and fabrics. . . from process to product!

Mary Anne Caplinger
1536 W. Horseshoe Bend
Rochester Hills, MI 48064

There are moments when I wonder how I moved or evolved in the direction of figures. I work very hard and sometimes more hours than I would like. . . but then I look around me and feel fortunate to have this sense of direction. There are so many people that have difficulty with the direction of their work . . .then the motivation to do the work.
Caty Carlin
1511 E. 7th
Charlotte, N.C. 28204

I enjoy machine embroidery for several reasons. One is that the sewing machine is a mechanical tool, and I tend to be a very mechanical person. Machine embroidery provides me with an opportunity to earn a living . . .working for, with and around others who share the common bond of a love for fabrics, threads and creativity. Not many people are fortunate enough to be employed doing something they really love. Last but not least . . . it's really fun!

Debbie Casteel
240 No. "I" St.
Livermore, CA 94550

Because I live in the Sierra Nevada mountains of California, my work often reflects a closeness to nature. I work with fiber, sometimes combining it with earth, shells, pebbles. Usually my art has an ancient, primal feeling. Perhaps this is why I feel comfortable with 'old' techniques like feltmaking, basketry, weaving and papermaking.

Kathleen Curtis
Box 10
Truckee, CA 95734

Right now I am doing only commissions. While I welcome the challenge of designing to specifications, I feel the need to take a break to do some experimental work in a new direction. I find that once agents have your slides, you are asked to do the old work again and again, instead of breaking new ground.

Working on these studies for your book has been fun and it did make me try some new ideas and expand on old ones. Thanks for including me.

Ardi Davis
Rt. 2 Box 99F
Leesburg, VA 22075

I find an inner joy and sense of being . . in my creative work.

Jo Anne Dougherty
1903 Brewster Ave.
Redwood City, CA 94062

Few artists start out as papermakers. Most come from painting, sculpture, or printmaking. I am primarily a painter who discovered that effects can be achieved with hand manipulated paper pulp, that would otherwise require endless re-working of a canvas. I continue to explore these possibilities.

My themes are primarily related to ecology, to our use and abuse of the environment.

Ingrid Evans
2165 Driscoll Drive
Reno, NV 89509

I love the endless possibilities that I see in cloth . . . . it's a never ending dialogue between me and my piles of textures and colors. I play with any materials to create a visual spontaneity of line and color like the ease of drawing at my fingertips.

Diane Ericson Frode
Box 349
Tahoe City, CA 95730

As a member of the human race and an artist, I am right now, using fabric as raw material to express my ideas. There exists a kind of dialogue with the material: it does the talking and I listen and respond.

My work with fabric is in two different areas, contemporary. wall pieces and ecclesiastical commissions. I take the symbolism and distill the essence through my personal relationship to ideas. The piece becomes the rapport between myself and the person or space for which it was created. All pieces are a form of communication. I hope to evoke a response from the viewer: an involvement with the ideas, on some level of excitement, understanding or renewal.

Emelyn Garafolo
56 William St.
Copiague, NY 11726

I see my photography as a challenge to look beyond the object, past my first impression to the least obvious solution.

It was interesting, for me, to take the inspirational photos and then to see the form of the interpretations return to a picture in the end.

Laura Gregersen
2000 Deer Run
Carson City, NV 89701

There is a difference between knowing and finding out. Exploring the use of materials, allowing the image to emerge without forcing . . interests me. My work is like a safari. The surprises are enjoyable. They give me a new way of seeing. They offer directions for further work. When I work from the heart . . intuition and emotion follow. They lead, my hands are the tools. I try to trust my feelings for when I do the work is successful for me and produces a like response from the viewer. I like to find out.

Gayle Luchessa
4107 Shelter Bay Ave.
Mill Valley, CA 94941

I'm primarily a surface designer, but I have come to realize that texture is integral in my work. I prefer to work with more sculptural fabrics (corduroy, velveteen) and I often quilt or embroider on the finished fabric. Fiber manipulation seems a natural, logical step forward. I'm beginning to see manipulation as another way of creating pattern, where instead of dye and paint, light and shadow form the design. I'm intrigued by the possibilities of combining paint/dye/print with pleat/cut/fold. I've barely begun to imagine what could grow out of the two together.

Karen Perrine
512 No. 'K' St.
Tacoma, WA 98403

I believe creating something special and artful in which to clothe the body is not a trivial thing. The body is home to our spiritual essence. The challenge to make something wonderful with limited resources . . .forces me, an artist, to look within and to say who I am. I am guided by a theme or storyline in the design process. Color and texture, things for the eye to 'grasp' are also key elements. I want to create a tangible YES, to meld theme, color and texture in a positive way. I want you to smile and feel good about yourself when you wear what I've created.

Mary Preston
705 N. Carr
Tacoma, WA 98403

Since I've been making paper, I find that my work has taken on a spontaneity that is amazing to me. It is the most exciting medium I've worked with, to date. Experimenting with color, shape, and the inherent qualities of paper is very important in my daily work.

I am totally influenced by nature . . . the beauty of shells, geodes, feathers, a morning sunrise over Lake Tahoe, geese flying overhead. . . these artistic and lovely images help me to cope with the heavy man-made problems of this precious, fragile world.

Barbi Racich
Box EE
Tahoe City, CA 95730

As a fiber artist, I find it exciting to explore new ways to use the medium. Fabric manipulation, painting, screenprinting, and embellishment give me endless possibilities for creating new designs.

Linda Kimura Rees
8029 S. Lakeridge Dr.
Seattle, WA 98178

My major interest is working with color and color relationships. I am also fascinated with line and rhythm. Achieving the illusion of luminosity and three-dimensionality within a two-dimensional format is also of interest. For me, strip piecing has been an ideal medium, particularly since I love working with fabric and have a passion for quilts.

Laura Munson Reinstatler
Box 85145
Seattle, WA 98145

My degree in painting and graphics laid a background for my continual discovery of the possibilities of machine embroidery as an art form. Over the 11 years I have developed and learned techniques to create textures and lines unique to the machine. Teaching for stores, guilds, and other sewing enthusiasts promotes creativity for my students and myself.

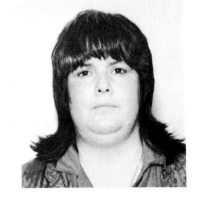

Pat Rodgers
Box 3022
Huntington, NY 11743

Do I ever love texture! I'm forever running my hands over objects so that I can 'know' them better. Since I personally need a lot of visual stimulation, I tend to put a lot of objects in my work. Never having been known as the shy, retiring type, I guess my work reflects my personality . . . sort of the 'run you over and then back up to make sure you noticed' school of art. How history will treat my efforts I probably won't be around to see, but I do know that the sweet intensity that I feel when I'm creating is something that I can't get enough of. Most of the time, that joy I feel while working is enough to keep me going.

Nancy Smeltzer
9822 Pushcart Way
Columbia, MD 21045

I love translating buildings, nature and feelings into fabric pieces. Although I have never considered myself an artist, I am often surprised and delighted with what my sewing machine and I produce. I'll never run out of ideas.

Lois Smith
4821 Bel Pre Rd.
Rockville, MD 20853

The purity of the Japanese aesthetic speaks very strongly to me. The concept of 'less is more' to express one's feelings is my challenge. My interest in calligraphy and meditation influence my approach, guiding me toward my own expression of the incredible order of our universe.

Mary Street
Box 6826
Tahoe City, CA 95730

Using fabric and thread, many different theses occur in my works which are designed to challenge the viewer's way of thinking. Significantly, each piece demonstrates interaction between color, motion, and texture. I strive for my art to reflect concepts which are apparent in daily existence: order in a chaotic world, color in a pale world, and beauty in an imperfect world.

Lynne Sward
625 Bishop St.
Virginia Beach, VA 23455

For the last 15 years, it has been my major fascination in my work to experiment with different dyes on natural fibers--on cotton, silk and paper. After a long period of concentrating solely on surface design, I progressed into more sculptural forms. The chief joy to me is to see the way that the light reflects and shines through a piece. Fiber is a very cooperative medium. It is pliant and strong at the same time. It is wonderful to me that whenever I am working on a piece, it always results in ideas I want to try next. From the fantastic variety of work that I have seen in fiber shows during the last few years, I conclude that fiber holds the same fascination for a vast number of other people, too.

Anne Syer
653 Bianco Ct.
Davis, CA 95616

Working with the materials gathered for this book has been a challenge and the opportunity to work with its author a pleasure.

Linda Taynahza
Box 1886
Truckee, CA 95734

Since I entered the world of quilting 3 years ago, I've been busy learning about and experimenting with the world of color and design with fabrics through workshops, books, observing nature, etc. It's a constant learning experience and I find it very exciting.

Liz Thoman
956 - 178th Ave. N.E.
Seattle, WA 98008

I used to be a sculptor, but my love for fabric, color and texture--along with a facility for sewing--led me down a one way path: textile art. There's no going any other direction for me. I love what I'm doing: wearable art, contemporary quilts, fabric manipulation. It's hard to make choices just within this field, though. I want to do everything--at once!

Lorraine Torrence
2112 So. Spokane St.
Seattle, WA 98144

After seeing my work and my books . . . a lady that I met said "My, you sure are lucky!"

I said, "Yes, I know . . .I find the harder I work, the luckier I get."

Just because one is sooooo deserving . . . opportunities (it would seem) would just fall in one's lap. All we have to do is <u>wait.</u>

Personally, I love to work. . . . My work is necessary for my life . . . it helps me to grow, it sustains me, it causes me to remain open and in turn receiving . . . helps me to give . . . . Nothing is too much trouble. (Well, almost nothing.)

Lois Ericson
Box 1680
Tahoe City, CA 95730

bibliography

Adachi, Fumie; Translator. JAPANESE DESIGN MOTIFS, Dover Publ., N.Y.; 1972.

Bullock, Wynn. PHOTOGRAPHY: A WAY OF LIFE, Morgan & Morgan Publ., Dobbs Ferry, N.Y. ; 1977.

Diringer, David. THE BOOK BEFORE PRINTING, Dover Publ., N.Y.; 1982.

Embroidery Guild. NEEDLEWORK SCHOOL, Chartwell Books, Inc.; 1984.

Fanning, Robbie and Tony. THE COMPLETE BOOK OF MACHINE EMBROIDERY, Chilton Book Co., Radnor, PA; 1986.

Gardiner, Stephen. INSIDE ARCHITECTURE, Prentice-Hall, Inc., N.J.; 1983.

Gordon, Beverly. FELTMAKING, Watson-Guptill Publ., N.Y.; 1980.

Green, Louise. FELTMAKING: INSTANT DELIGHT, Interweave, Vol. III. No.4, Summer, 1978.

Green, Louise. FELTMAKING FOR THE FIBER ARTIST, Greentree Ranch Wools, 163 N. Carter Lake Rd., Loveland, CO 80537

Grunebaum, Gabriele. HOW TO MARBELIZE PAPER, Dover Publ., Inc., N.Y.; 1984.

Haeckel, Ernst. ART FORMS IN NATURE, Dover Publ., N.Y.; 1974.

Howard, Constance. EMBROIDERY AND COLOR, B.T. Batsford Ltd., London; 1986.

Hunter, Dard. PAPERMAKING, Dover Publ., N.Y.; 1978.

Messent, Jan. EMBROIDERY AND NATURE, B.T. Batsford Ltd., London; 1984.

Proctor, Richard and Jennifer Lew. SURFACE DESIGN FOR FABRIC, University of Washington Press, Seattle, WA; 1984.

Rhodes, Zandra and Anne Knight. THE ART OF ZANDRA RHODES, Houghton Mifflin Co., Boston; 1985.

Sommer, Elyse and Mike. A NEW LOOK AT FELT, Crown Publications, N.Y.; 1975.

Warren, Verina. LANDSCAPE IN EMBROIDERY, B.T. Batsford Ltd., London; 1986.

suppliers

Aardvark Adventures
Box 2449
Livermore, CA 94550

Beads, threads, 'solvy' (stabilizer) sample catalog $1.00

Color Craft, Ltd.
Box 936
Avon, CT 06001

Createx Color, catalog . . . free

Paper Source
1506 W. 12th St.
Los Angeles, CA 90015

Supplies for papermaking, catalog $3.00

Skyloom Studio
Jackson Brockette
1715 Mapleton Dr.
Dallas, TX 75228

Marbeling Dust $12.00 for 1/2 lb. makes 45 qts of solution; price includes postage

Straw into Gold
3006 San Pablo Ave.
Berkeley, CA 94702

Dyes, seagrass, silk raffia; catalog $1.50

Twinrocker, Inc.
RFD 2
Brookson, IN 47923

Papermaking supplies, linters, sizing

Lois Ericson
Box 1680
Tahoe City, CA 95730

Pleaters ... will make traditional or contemporary smocking fun and easy. Write for current price list.

Books available:
DESIGN & SEW IT YOURSELF $14.95
BELTS ... WAISTED SCULPTURE $13.95
FABRICS ... RECONSTRUCTED $11.95

P&H $1.50 for 1 to 3 books - CA res. add 6%
Wholesale 40%, 12 or more
Canada Postal MO only

index

a

Adams, B.J., 16, 24, 34, 85, 98,
   136, 137, 138, 139, 209
Applique, 141, 144, 145, 146,
   147
Artists, 207

b

Barbed wire, 44
Beading, 146, 147
Bibliography, 221
Box, 151, 176
Brick building, 38
Brockette, Jackson, 169
Buttons, 126
Buzz words, 205

c

Caplinger, Mary Ann, 74, 209
Carlin, Caty, 13, 23, 82, 91,
   141, 209
Cars, 80
Casteel, Debbie, 151, 210
Chapter preview, 8, 105, 178,
   208
Church steeple, 20
Content, 5
Cord, 150
Cording, 112, 113, 172, 188
Cornice, 58
Couching, 120, 121, 176
Curtis, Kathleen, 160, 161, 210
Cut shapes, 22

d

Davis, Ardi, 14, 40, 97, 122,
   123, 124, 125, 211
Dedication, 2
Dougherty, JoAnne, 148, 149,
   211
Draped, 35

e

Elastic thread, 69, 134, 135
Empty garments, 166, 167
Ericson, Lois, 35, 41, 48, 56,
   61, 62, 90, 94, 99,
   166, 167, 168, 169,
   170, 171, 172, 173, 174,
   175, 219
Evans, Ingrid, 75, 156, 157, 102,
   211

f

Faced shapes, 48, 138, 139,
   190, 191, 192, 193
Felting, 160, 161, 205
Fleece, 56
Folded, 40
   Accordians, 14
   Painted, 13
   Stitched, 122, 123
   Strips, 108, 109
Foreword, 4
Fringe, 68, 154, 155
Frode, Diane Ericson, 126, 127,
   101, 212

g

Garafolo, Emelyn, 15, 86, 88,
   104, 106, 107, 108, 109,
   110, 111, 112
Gregersen, Laura, 1, 212

h, i

Ideas, quote, 3
Inset shapes, 126, 127, 194
Introduction, 6

j, k, l

Leaves, 50
Luchessa, Gayle, 92, 162, 163,
   164, 165, 213

m, n

Machine embroidery, 53, 67,
   142, 143, 151
Manipulated tucks, 138, 139,
   172, 173, 177, 186, 187
Marbeling, 148, 149, 169, 202,
   203
Milkweed pod, 64

o, p

Painting, 13, 40, 46, 48, 74, 75, 82, 118, 119, 121, 124, 125, 126, 127
Paper, 13, 52, 54, 70, 75, 156, 157, 158, 159, 204
Perrine, Karen, 12, 32, 33, 130, 131, 132, 133, 213
Piecing, 17, 26, 27, 62, 66, 76, 77, 116, 117, 134, 135, 141, 144, 145, 169, 182
Piping, 82, 112, 113, 140, 189

Plato, 3
Pleated, 16, 41, 124, 125, 130, 131, 132, 133, 136, 137
Pleats, 12, 18, 83, 85, 136, 137
Preston, Mary, 60, 78, 84, 95, 118, 119, 120, 121, 213
Process, 7

q

Quilting, 17, 26, 27, 28, 46, 66, 76, 116, 117, 118, 134, 135, 144, 145, 146, 147, 148, 149
Quotes, 3, 224

r

Racich, Barbi, 52, 70, 93, 158, 159, 214
Radiators, 10
Rees, Linda Kimura, 25, 55, 128, 129, 214
Reinstatler, Laura, 17, 26, 27, 66, 76, 96, 116, 117, 215
Rock wall, 72
Rodgers, Pat, 36, 53, 67, 142, 143, 215
Rolled buttons, 126
Rolled paper, 13, 152, 153

s

Serged edges, 86, 106, 107, 110, 111, 168, 174, 175
Shirring, 82, 195

Smeltzer, Nancy, 47, 100, 144, 145, 146, 147, 215
Smith, Lois, 28, 69, 83, 134, 135, 216
Smocking, 16, 34, 196, 197
Stabilizer, 53, 201
Statue, 30
Street, Mary, 46, 150, 216
Stitching, 24, 28, 32, 35, 36, 41, 47, 55, 56, 60, 84, 85, 106, 108, 109, 114, 115, 118, 119, 120, 121, 120, 142, 184, 185
Suppliers, 220
Sward, Lynne, 22, 89, 114, 115, 216
Syer, Anne, 13, 54, 68, 77, 152, 153, 154, 155, 217

t

Taynahza, Linda, 1, 217
Techniques, 179
Thoman, Liz, 82, 140, 218
Torrance, Lorraine, 18, 42, 112, 113, 218
Tubes, 23, 61, 82, 83, 86, 170, 171, 198, 199, 200
Tucks, 12, 18, 24, 25, 28, 42, 62, 82, 128, 129, 136, 137, 138, 129, 172, 173, 177, 186, 187

u, v, w

Weaving, 74, 174, 175
Wires, 44, 164, 165
Words, 205
Work, 103
Wrapped buttons, 126, 127
Wrinkled stitched, 15, 84, 180, 181

x, y, z

Zarbaugh, Jerry, 4

One of my favorite quotes . . . thought you might 'need' it, too.

"For a long time it had seemed that life was about to begin . . . REAL LIFE. But there was always some obstacle in the way. Something to get through first. Some unfinished business . . . time still to be served. A debt to be paid.

THEN life would begin. At last it dawned on me that these obstacles were my life."

Alfred D'Souza